"Only those who have suffered are trfering of others. And only those wh and healing are capable of sharing i Shelly and Wanda have written a be ing book, bringing beauty from the asnes u. painful stories."

—**KATHIE LEE GIFFORD**, Cohost of the fourth hour of the *Today Show*

"This book is a gift. In over twenty years of women's ministry, I have met a lot of hurting women who have needed a resource like this. I'm thrilled to be able to offer them the rich truth found on these pages."

—**JILL SAVAGE**, CEO of Hearts at Home, author of nine books including *Real Moms . . . Real Jesus* and *No More Perfect Moms*

"One of the worst feelings in the world is the feeling of being all alone, carrying a secret you fear no one would understand. *Love Letters from the Edge* assures us that we are not alone; God understands. Let this book voice for you the unspoken pain that runs silent and deep. And then in its pages hear the tender and comforting replies of the Father who wants each of us to know that we are cherished and adored."

—**STEVE SILER**, Founder and director of Music for the Soul

"*Love Letters from the Edge* is a welcome addition to the spiritual journey of healing. Let us pray that many will experience the gift within these pages."

—**DR. ALVEDA C. KING**, Executive director of African American Outreach, Priests for Life

"The authors have experienced what it's like to fall into the dark places in life, and they have used their healing to minister to thousands of hurting women. More than just meditations, Shelly and Wanda offer practical guidance and encouragement, and subtly whisper, 'Open yourself to God's healing—as we did.'"

—**CECIL MURPHEY**, author or coauthor of 135 books, including *90 Minutes in Heaven* and *Gifted Hands: The Ben Carson Story*

"With startling and intimate conversations with God, you will think Shelly Beach and Wanda Sanchez have been eavesdropping on your most secret thoughts. They describe the pain, fear, shame, and regret we all feel at times and all the ways we try to hide. But this powerful book brings hope for despair. God himself supplies a healing balm through the tender words and gentle assurances found in Scripture. You'll be equipped with practical steps to move from hopelessness, fear, and doubt to live in the reality of God's restoration and healing hope. This is a powerful book you will share with many."

—**NANCY STAFFORD**, Actress, speaker, and author of
The Wonder of His Love: A Journey into the Heart of God
and *Beauty by the Book: Seeing Yourself as God Sees You*

"This is a must-read for anyone who has ever been hurt or suffered traumatic loss. Not only do Sanchez and Beach share hard truths with depth and compassion, but as survivors of tremendous pain in their own journeys, they deliver a message of hope with authenticity and empathy unlike any other. In this book, they have bravely combined their tremendous talents to help heal other wounded spirits and soothe even the deepest scars.

—**JULIE CANTRELL**, *New York Times* and *USA TODAY* best-selling author of *Into the Free* and *When Mountains Move*

"Each person's journey is unique, but one thing's for sure—this book can provide one form of that much-needed loving support . . . Sure to touch the hearts of the hurting and to promote healing in their lives."

—**GRACE FOX**, National codirector of International Messengers Canada and author of *Moving from Fear to Freedom: A Woman's Guide to Peace in Every Situation*

"The inspirational words in *Love Letters from the Edge* touch the deepest wounds in a broken woman's heart and demonstrate God's unconditional love and healing for His daughters."

—**MEL & ANNIE GOEBEL**, Founder-CEO and president of Daughters of Destiny, www.daughtersofdestiny.org

"The honesty with which the authors approach difficult situations comes only from those who have walked through deep waters. Time after time I was moved to tears followed by an overwhelming sense of God's presence as the authors move into words of assurance from the heavenly Father. This is a book I will read often and share with the women who come to Dégagé in the midst of life's storms and struggles. There is no greater gift to give someone than the gift of hope in a heavenly Father who loves them unconditionally."

—**MARGE PALMERLEE**, Executive director of Dégagé Ministries

"Through a balanced message of truth and grace Shelley and Wanda have created an invaluable gift for those who have experienced significant trauma, disappointment, and loss. The reader will gain notable insights into the impact of trauma, helpful tools that will enable those affected by trauma to regain emotional and relational health, and wise counsel about how the development of one's spiritual life can help turn tragedy into triumph over time."

—**SAM BEALS**, President and CEO of Wedgewood Christian Services

"Shelly Beach and Wanda Sanchez, out of their own painful journeys, have made it abundantly clear that God is available for hurting people. *Love Letters from the Edge* will pull us back from the edge when we wonder if God really cares about the deep struggles we're going through. To some degree, we've all been dangerously close to that edge of wondering if there's hope. Whether that time of life is called brokenness, trauma, or pain, we've all been there. These two authors affirm clearly that God is near and keeps His promise to never forsake or abandon us. I'm so glad this is available."

—**KATHY COLLARD MILLER**, speaker and author of many books, including *Partly Cloudy with Scattered Worries*

"*Love Letters from the Edge* is poignant, gripping, and soul stirring. This book is a must-read for survivors of abuse and trauma who feel like God abandoned them. The authors insightfully allow readers to discover the many ways God has walked with them through a painful journey. Because the authors have experienced trauma, abuse, and abandonment, they write with perceptive understanding of the journey of healing."

—**DR. BETH ROBINSON**, Professor of counseling,
Lubbock Christian University

"*Love Letters from the Edge* is a gift to all who struggle with the brokenness of life. The authors understand our pain. They give truth and hope as they help us know we're never alone in the valley of suffering and trauma."

—**GARY HEIM**, Pastor, author, and counselor

"*Love Letters from the Edge* contains some of the most wise, frank, and courageous prayers you will ever read. Those who've survived trauma, abuse, or the pain of loss will recognize their own emotions, struggles, and questions mirrored in the words of this book. But this is not a one-way heaven-aimed monologue. Shelly Beach and Wanda Sanchez invite survivors into a two-way conversation with the Lord of love. . . . The kind of love letter that can speak into the deepest crevices of a hurting heart. Highly recommended."

—**MICHELLE VAN LOON**, author of *If Only: Letting Go of Regret*

LOVE
LETTERS
from the
EDGE

MEDITATIONS *for* THOSE STRUGGLING *with* BROKENNESS,
TRAUMA, *and the* PAIN *of* LIFE

SHELLY BEACH *and* WANDA SANCHEZ

Love Letters from the Edge: Meditations for Those Struggling with Brokenness, Trauma, and the Pain of Life
© 2014 by Shelly Beach and Wanda Sanchez

Published by Kregel Publications, a division of Kregel, Inc., 2450 Oak Industrial Drive NE, Grand Rapids, MI 49505

The authors and publisher are not engaged in rendering medical or psychological services, and this book is not intended as a guide to diagnose or treat medical or psychological problems. If medical, psychological, or other expert assistance is required by the reader, please seek the services of your own health care provider or certified counselor.

ISBN 978-0-8254-4347-3

Printed in the United States of America
14 15 16 17 18 / 5 4 3 2 1

To my dad,
Who taught me to love God, truth, and family,
and what it looks like to live gratefully.
—Shelly Beach

To Grandma, thank you for everything,
and to Auntie Emily, my hero, who taught me to dream
and to love books and words.
—Wanda Sanchez

Contents

Grieving and Growing
Will it ever be better, God?

Hope and a Future
Can you redeem this pain, God?

Love and Assurance
Can you say it again, God?

Introduction

Adversity introduces a man to himself.
UNKNOWN

Not long ago, my friend Wanda and I threw a party for Christian women in leadership from across the nation. We invited award-winning authors, filmmakers, speakers, agents, and people in Christian media to come and network about influencing culture for God's kingdom.

As Wanda and I surveyed our friends that evening, we noted one overwhelming characteristic. The vast majority of the women had experienced life-changing trauma at some point: sexual abuse, domestic violence, rape, arson, family suicide, even the attempted murder of a family member and murder of a child. Other women had lost loved ones in tragic accidents, experienced medical trauma, or had been touched by other life-altering tragedies.

Of the sixteen women at the event, at least five (31%) were suffering from or at one time had suffered from severe and ongoing symptoms of post-traumatic stress disorder (PTSD). At least four others (25%) had experienced PTSD symptoms that had made it difficult to cope with life for more than a year. Simple math told us that trauma and the aftereffects of PTSD had dramatically influenced more than 50 percent of the women in the room. Including us, the authors of this book.

When I was nineteen years old, I (Shelly) was attacked by the most prolific serial rapist in a tristate area. His assault forever changed my life, and while that experience was horrifically painful, God used it to teach me things about himself that radically changed my view of my purpose in life and my relationship to the world. My dear friend and coauthor Wanda Sanchez was placed in a broken county juvenile system when her young parents were incarcerated. Abuse ravaged her life, and for years she struggled with the symptoms of PTSD. But Wanda's mother and father came to know Jesus in prison, and today Wanda's family relationships are healed.

To the uninformed, it might appear that our friends and Wanda and I have led unusually traumatic lives; however, the 2010 National Intimate Partner and Sexual Violence Survey (NISVS) reports that nearly one in five women in the United States have been raped, one in four have been the victim of physical violence by an intimate partner, and one out of six women have been stalked.[1] Of the women present at our gathering, 44 percent had been sexually abused. According to a study published in the *American Journal of Preventive Medicine*, one in four girls (25%) are sexually abused by the age of eighteen, and one in six boys (16%) are sexually abused by the age of eighteen.[2] Interestingly, at least 25 percent of the women gathered for our event had been sexually abused before the age of eighteen. Additionally, the National Coalition Against Domestic Violence reports that one in

---

1. M. C. Black et al., "National Intimate Partner and Sexual Violence Survey: 2010 Summary Report," National Center for Injury Prevention and Control, Centers for Disease Control and Prevention, November 2011, http://www.cdc.gov/violenceprevention/pdf/nisvs_executive_summary-a.pdf.

2. S. R. Dube et al., "Long-Term Consequences of Childhood Sexual Abuse by Gender of Victim," *American Journal of Preventive Medicine* 28, no. 5 (June 2005): 430–38, http://www.ncbi.nlm.nih.gov/pubmed/15894146?dopt=Abstract.

four women will experience domestic violence in her lifetime.[3] Again, 25 percent of our group of friends—Christian women in positions of leadership—had experienced domestic violence.

Chances are that whoever you are, you or someone you know and love has been affected by trauma—the yucky, painful "junk" of life. If that person is you, those experiences have very likely taken you to deep places of suffering and loss. It's also likely you've seldom, if ever, spoken to others about the depth of your pain, your sense of isolation, and your feelings of abandonment.

You may have been hurt—victimized—at the hands of others. Perhaps once. Perhaps many times. The pain of those traumas cuts deeply into your soul and often leaves lifetime scars.

Unfortunately, those who experience trauma often don't understand that the deeply painful experiences that overwhelm us produce biological and chemical consequences as well as spiritual and emotional consequences. One's body chemistry does not end at the neck, and the same chemicals that influence the liver, kidneys, and heart also influence cells and blood vessels in the brain. Trauma creates lasting and profound symptoms defined as post-traumatic stress disorder (PTSD). Unfortunately, people often wrongly think that PTSD affects only combat veterans or those who have experienced mass disasters like 9/11.

They're wrong. The effects of trauma can have lasting and lifelong effects on those who have experienced invasive or early childhood medical procedures, the separation of adoption, domestic violence, sexual abuse, devastating accidents, the death of loved ones, natural disasters, and other painful losses. Traumatologist Margaret Vasquez,

---

3. "Domestic Violence Facts," National Coalition Against Domestic Violence, accessed October 1, 2013, http://www.ncadv.org/files/Domestic ViolenceFactSheet%28National%29.pdf.

certified trauma therapist and certified intensive trauma therapy instructor with Kairos Trauma Consultants, defines trauma as any event that overwhelms an individual's ability to cope. Perhaps you have become overwhelmed by the spiritual, emotional, and physical consequences of traumatic events in your life because you don't know where to turn.

We know your struggle. We know the face of trauma, post-traumatic stress disorder, confusion, and desperation because those struggles have been our own. We are here to tell you that even in the depths of your deepest despair, God hears your cries, and you have reason to hope.

Over the past several years, Wanda and I have traveled tens of thousands of miles across the nation and spoken to women in churches both large and small, as well as at prisons, hospitals, and mental health facilities. No matter where we speak, the needs of women are the same: they need hope in despair and to know that there is healing for their brokenness. The devotionals in this book reflect the stories of hundreds of these women, as well as our own.

This book of meditations is different from many others. It's written from two perspectives. The first half of each entry is a letter from the brokenhearted to her Father God. The second half is God's love letter of response to his wounded child who has been hurt by sexual abuse, violence, abandonment, victimization, or other painful life issues. It's our prayer that *Love Letters from the Edge* will become a message of consolation, comfort, and hope on your journey to healing—a message of love from God's heart to yours.

—*Shelly Beach and Wanda Sanchez*

How to Use This Book

Love Letters from the Edge is a twelve-week book of meditations designed to help you express your questions and frustrations to God and to better understand his heart for you. The book also offers tools that give you an overview of post-traumatic stress disorder. Activities include journaling questions, letter writing, art projects, and other activities designed to help you move toward healing and deepen your relationship with God.

The appendixes at the back of the book include information that will help you better understand and access helpful information on PTSD and its symptoms. We've included websites, assessment tests, treatment centers, Scripture affirmations, and suggestions for friends, spouses, and the church, as well as other resources.

As the authors of this book, we must state that we're not therapists. If you're experiencing symptoms that can accompany trauma and post-traumatic stress disorder—depression, suicidal thoughts, self-abuse, or other mental health issues—we encourage you to consult a mental health professional. Reading about and writing about your memories and experiences can be potential triggers for trauma symptoms, such as anxiety, depression, or self-harm.

We encourage you to purchase a writing journal and an art notebook and to complete as many of the activities as you feel are appropriate to your needs. If you are working with a counselor or therapist, be sure to consult them about the activities you undertake.

If you suspect you have PTSD and have never sought treatment from a traumatologist, we suggest you prayerfully seek the help of a professional qualified in treating the psychological aspects of trauma that influence the processing functions of the brain. Trauma treatment is vastly different from counseling, and addresses the biological wiring that is altered when traumatic experiences overwhelm the brain. It is important to remember that all truth belongs to God, and a division between "secular" and "sacred" is a false division. PTSD influences the body, mind, and spirit, and a comprehensive treatment plan should integrate the best medical treatment with biblical truth.

You are about to embark on a spiritual journey of discovery and change. Expect opposition. Satan does not want you to find freedom. He does not want you to be well. We encourage you to ask close friends and loved ones to pray for you and we encourage you to find a trusted, discerning companion for your journey.

Be encouraged with this truth: God loves you more passionately than you could ever comprehend. He has come for you, and he will never leave you—no matter what your emotions may tell you or where life may find you.

He gave what he loved most to rescue you: his Son.

In this very moment, he is whispering to you: *Come to me. You are loved.*

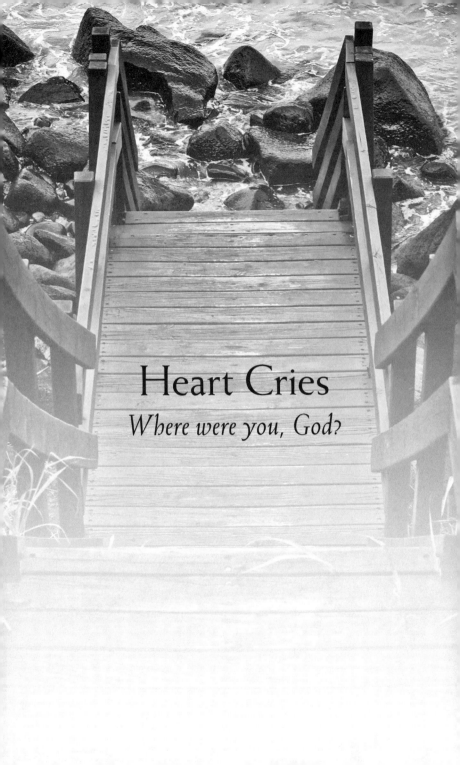

Heart Cries

Where were you, God?

WEEK ONE

I see you and know you.

My Precious One,
I am close to the brokenhearted
and save the crushed in spirit.

—YOUR FATHER
FROM PSALM 34:18

Where Were You?

Have I not commanded you? Be strong and courageous.
Do not be frightened, and do not be dismayed, for the LORD
your God is with you wherever you go.

God,

When I was a little girl, someone told me it was wrong to get mad at you, or to ask you questions. But that doesn't make sense to me.

Since you're God, I figure you must know everything I'm thinking and feeling, when things are good or when they're awful. And if you're truly a father who loves me in the good times and in the bad, you want me to bring you my tough questions because I don't need you very much for the easy ones.

So where were you, God, when all the horrible things in life were happening to me? Where were you in the moments when I felt abandoned and alone? I prayed a thousand times for the torture to stop, but the nightmare happened over and over, again and again until my heart shriveled up inside of me and my prayers stuck in my throat.

I waited for you to rescue me. I prayed and I prayed, but the hurt kept coming. As the years passed, I tried to keep believing you cared.

With one wave of your finger, you parted the Red Sea for the children of Israel. But you didn't come for me.

You saved Daniel in the lions' den. But you didn't save me.

You freed Paul from his prison cell. But you didn't free me.

Where were you, God? Wasn't I important enough? Was I just too bad—the one person who wasn't worth it? Other people I loved suffered, too. I did everything I could to protect them and sacrifice myself so they wouldn't suffer.

For years I prayed you'd send someone to rescue me—to rescue us.

Even in the years when I tried to convince myself you weren't there or were a monster who didn't care, I never really stopped asking you to come.

Will you come for me now?

My Beloved Child,

It's all right if you have questions. I understand why the world doesn't make sense to you, and I understand your anger, rage, and pain. I have never taken my eyes off you for an instant. But as you come to know me better, you will understand that trying to understand answers beyond your comprehension is less important than trusting my character.

I want nothing more than for my children to be whole and well, but the world you live in is sick. Earthly wholeness is impossible. The pain and torture you experienced were caused by the sinful actions of humans exercising their choice and free will. And although I did not override their choices, I was with you, and you have been rescued in ways you cannot see and often look beyond.

Rescue is not always taking out and taking away. Rescue also comes in gifts of presence, endurance, transcendence, and purpose.

You didn't see me. You didn't hear me. And you didn't feel me in every moment of pain. But I was always beside you, holding you close to my heart, loving you, and wiping away every tear.

Know that I promise justice, although in this life you will not see the final pages of that chapter written.

I love you with a pure love that exceeds the limits of earthly understanding. Don't give up, my daughter. Healing and wholeness are available to you and are being written into your story even now.

I came for you, and I have never left your side. Reach out, and you will find me here.

Hope on the Edge

When have you asked God to rescue you? Did God's silence ever feel like abandonment to you? How did you handle those feelings?

How have you reconciled faith in a loving, sovereign God with the hurt you've experienced in your life?

Heart Cry

Dear Father, help me believe I'm not without hope, that I'm not unloved, that I'm not abandoned. Help me see who you really are and that my pain does not define your love. Help me understand that answers will never be enough and that your love and character alone are all I can trust in—no matter what I may feel.

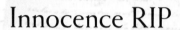

Innocence RIP

*Jesus said, "Let the little children come to me, and do not hinder
them, for the kingdom of heaven belongs to such as these.*
MATTHEW 19:14

Dear God,

In three notes, a song on the radio takes me hostage, and in a
heartbeat, I'm thrown onto the roller coaster of sad-and-angry-and-
terrified-and-sad.

Up and down, feelings fly as I'm tossed around turns of memory.
I'm back *there*—reliving the childhood nightmare. The moment I
give in to the surge of sadness, my stomach drops, and the rush of
rage comes—rage that I was robbed.

But not just robbed. My innocence and childhood were stolen.
Triggers, flashbacks, and nightmares own my life. And whenever
I tiptoe up to the memory and think about the moment my world
changed forever and part of me died, my spirit shatters into a million
pieces.

Empty.   Afraid.

            Hopeless.
                                    Used.

Angry.   Forgotten.

                              Abandoned.

I'm sad that part of me disappeared and so few people ever mourned for the lost and empty child. I'm sad beyond words for the precious, irretrievable things that were stolen: A sense of protection and safety. The knowledge that I'm seen and heard. The feeling that I'm loved and wanted. The ability to trust. The confidence to love myself.

Those things were ripped from my hands like they were never mine. Will I ever get over the anger and sadness for their loss, for the death of my childhood?

You are God over all things, and I pray you can use something in this mess for good I can't see. But tonight, please hold the shattered child in me whose heart still cries for lost things.

Dearest Child of Mine,

As your Father, I treasure the trust you place in me when you share your heart—especially your doubts and fears. Yes, I know you hurt deeply, my child, and I carry your wounds inside my own heart. Although you have not always felt it, I have carried you through your deepest pain.

Even though it's difficult for you to trust what you cannot see, I can promise that I am using the tangled mess of your life in ways you cannot imagine. The glory that will come from the pain will ripple out into the scope of history for generations to come. Although you do not see it, your faith is breaking the chains of bondage in your family and setting free those you will not meet until eternity. In spite of all the things that have happened to you, overwhelming victory is yours through Jesus.

You're right, my daughter—your innocence was stolen, and those responsible will face me. But I will restore more than was taken from you and sow blessing into your future. Jesus came to restore your innocence and give you back your childhood. Rest assured, my child, no matter what you may feel, you are wrapped in my love, and you walk in heaven-bought innocence and purity. The full life that you desire exists as you live and breathe and find your being in Jesus.

Do not be troubled or afraid. I give power to the weak and strength to the powerless. Find new strength in me.

Hope on the Edge

What things have you lost that have brought you to "the edge" in life? How have you dealt with those losses?

What things are you asking God to restore? Can you envision ways that God can use your pain for blessing? How?

Heart Cry

Help me grieve what was lost. Give me a vision for who I am and the identity and inheritance that are mine through Jesus. My innocence is not lost, because Jesus bought it for me when he defeated sin. Thank you for giving back the things that were taken. Teach me to love like you love, God, and to see myself as the redeemed, beautiful daughter that you see.

Weeping in the Night

Away from me, all you who do evil,
for the LORD has heard my weeping.

PSALM 6:8

I can't sleep, God. I'm awake and exhausted, wide-eyed in the dark. Over and over again, my mind replays scenes I've lived and scenes I've made up—the endings I wish I could write to my story. Justice seems such a reasonable thing to ask for.

I'm angry. People hurt me in ways no one should ever be hurt— people who were supposed to love me and protect me.

But it didn't turn out that way.

Lord, I've tried to forget . . . tried to forgive. But night after night I lie alone in the dark with the voices and memories of the pain . . . images I can't erase. I remind myself I'm safe . . . that the monsters I fear are no longer part of my present. The problem is I still live in the shadows of my past.

If tears could flow, they would flood my pillow. I'm a lifetime of tired. I'm trying to push bricks back into the crumbling walls of my life, but they seem to fall out faster every day. My bones long for rest. My body and spirit beg for sleep. I want to close my eyes and not be afraid.

The evil that was poured out on my life sometimes feels like it's suffocating me. How long must I relive the memories, Lord?

In the darkness at night, I see the moon, and I know you hung it—that you're a God who's that big. Who's that powerful. Who's listening to me right now—even in my anger. I believe you're big enough for my questions and my hurt.

Please give me rest, Lord. I can't carry these burdens. My strength is gone, and I long for the day when I can lie down in peace and sleep.

My Dearest Child,

In those moments when a car suddenly flies out of control, a mother or father receives a dreaded diagnosis for a child, or feet suddenly slip from the edge of a cliff, the cry that flies without thought from the human heart is, "God!"—a cry for me. You are pressed beyond measure, dear one, and your spirit knows that only I can give you the rest you long for. You have come to me, and that simple act is your soul's deep worship and echoes through heaven as high praise.

I hear your cries, and I know your fears. I feel the ache of your body and hear the voices that pound through your soul. The weight of this world lies heavy on you.

Bring your fears to me.
   I have overcome the world. I am your safety.
Bring your anger to me.
   I have overcome the world. I am your reconciliation.
Bring the pain of your injustice to me.
   I have overcome the world. I am your recompense.
Bring your hopelessness to me.
   I have overcome the world. I am your hope.
Bring your anxiety to me.
   I have overcome the world. I am your peace.

In the darkness of night, I am the voice that sings over you in the silence.

The moon and all beautiful things I created remind you that I am always with you. Even now, I am giving you strength, sheltering and shielding you.

It is true. You are not alone. I wrote my promise to you in creation and signed it in the life and death of my Son. Be still and know that I am God.

Hope on the Edge

What worries and anxieties keep you awake in the night? What drives you to bring those things to God?

"God is your peace." What do those words mean to you? PTSD and other mental disorders can trap certain patterns of thinking in the mind. Consider memorizing some of the affirmations in appendix 6 at the back of the book, as well as seeking trauma treatment if you are experiencing sleep disturbances and obsessive thinking.

Heart Cry

Father, in the night when my heart and mind refuse to be quiet, remind me that you cradle me in your arms and hold me close to your heart. Your Spirit flows through me with every beat of my heart. Give me healing and peace as I focus on you and not my circumstances and feelings. Give me assurance of things I cannot see that are secure in you. Give me confidence that you will make all things right when I do not see justice. And give me rest, Lord, in body, mind, and spirit.

White Knights and Other Fairy Tales

Every good and perfect gift is from above,
coming down from the Father of the heavenly lights,
who does not change like shifting shadows.
JAMES 1:17

When I was a child, God, I heard about a princess named Cinderella, but I never understood why bad things happened to young girls in fairy tales. I knew Cinderella was beautiful and needed to be rescued from her sad life, but I wondered why she was abused and couldn't be loved and safe.

Eventually I read *Cinderella* to my baby sister and was awed by the girl who escaped from her abusers and rocked her world with a beautiful dress, shoes, pumpkin carriage, and a stunning prince. Most of all, I loved the rescue, God. Someone loved Cinderella enough to come after her and save her from her horrible life.

That's how I felt about the young, handsome marine I called Daddy. His uniform and shiny pins and medals fascinated me. He smelled good, had an easy smile, and I loved him. I knew I was safe when Daddy was around—like the day he sat on the floor and ate everything I made him in my Easy Bake Oven. He told me every dry little cake I gave him was wonderful, and I believed him.

But too often the smile I loved was missing, and a sad and tortured man looked back from Daddy's eyes. In the moments when my father drank and his focus drifted from me, I couldn't trust my world to be a safe place.

God, we are all children living in a fairy-tale-gone-wrong world of broken dreams. My father was a disappointed child once, too. Help me let go of the dream that imperfect people can keep me safe. Help me trust you to be my white knight and refuge. And give me grace to trust imperfect people with the same grace I need for my own imperfection.

Thank you most of all for restoring my father, who knows healing because of your grace.

My Child,

Your father was imperfect, like all earthly fathers, but you love him. It meant everything to you the day he sat on a hard floor and patiently waited while you served him everything your child hands could offer. That single act told you, more than anything else your father ever did, how much he cared for you. That day you felt safe and accepted as your daddy stooped down for his child. That day and many others, he showed you unconditional love.

But despite their best efforts, earthly fathers and mothers fail. Before eternity began, I set a story into motion for humanity, but they chose to rewrite it. The entire world is living in a story-gone-wrong. But my Son, Jesus, stepped into that story by becoming flesh and blood through a father-and-child relationship that will save the kingdom.

Your longings for safety are longings for me.

Your longings for a perfect father are longings for me.

Your longings for the prince on the white horse to save the kingdom are longings for me.

And I am here. For you. Trust me and a love that never changes, fades, or runs out.

Hope on the Edge

Who has failed you, and in what ways has your trust in people been challenged? How is God growing you in this area of your life?

What does it mean for you to trust people with the same grace you need in your imperfection?

Heart Cry

Dear God, help me see you as a father who picks me up and soothes away the nightmares. Help me understand that you are not a reflection of people who hurt me or let me down. You are the perfect, adoring, loving Father who is always watching over me. Help me love and trust you more.

A Place Called Desperation

So if the Son sets you free, you will be free indeed.
JOHN 8:36

O God,

Time and time I've tried to give it up and start over, but I've failed. After too many years, I've finally been forced to face the sad, sickening truth.

I'm a drug addict. A dope fiend. One of *those people.*

I believed drugs would change the way I felt. That they'd help me escape the awful place I was in and shed the pain. And they did—for a while. But somewhere along the way, they became one more thing that trapped me, and the thing I blindly hoped I could control ended up controlling me. The thing I told myself I *did* turned into the thing I *became.* Drugs took away my hope and destroyed my already chaotic life.

Drug addiction became one more thing that deepened the void in my life. One more thing that hurt me and the people I love. One more thing that drove me further into the darkness.

I'm angry at myself for believing I knew better than everyone else—for telling myself I wasn't like "other" addicts and that I wouldn't end up here. Angry for setting off to prove everyone wrong and myself right.

I feel beaten. I understand no drug in the world will fix me. But I'm trapped and can't see a way out.

I never thought I'd find myself in this desperate place. But I guess desperate is where I needed to land to realize I've got nowhere to run except to you.

First, dear one, understand that your salvation rests on your faith in Jesus, not on the things you do and don't do. Everything is permissible to you, unless that practice, substance, or person places you under bondage. You are not to be mastered by anything or allow anything to come before me. Drugs are an unforgiving master.

Don't lose hope, child. Some of my most beloved saints throughout history sank to the depths of hopelessness—Moses, David, and Elijah. What I desire from you is a moment-by-moment walk of faith as you rest in me. Addiction requires this kind of dependency as you grow in your awareness of your need for me in every moment.

Come to me, my weary and burdened child, and I will give you what you need most—rest for your soul. Allow me to search you and know you at your deepest point of need. I don't condemn you. Let me love you with a perfect love and give you the gifts of forgiveness, new life, and understanding. You were created for me and to be with me.

Fill the void inside you in sweet communion with me and be free.

Hope on the Edge
What addictions have you leaned on to fill the holes in your heart? How did these things influence your life and your relationships with those you love? In what ways have you sought help? You may want to consider checking out the resources of CelebrateRecovery.com.

What does it mean for you to turn to God to meet your needs in addiction—no matter what that addiction may look like?

Heart Cry

Dear Father, I relinquish the lie that I'm trapped and there's no way out. Free me from fear and teach me dependence upon you as I pry my hands off my life. Give me courage to be transparent and to seek out accountability and resources. Give grace to my family and loved ones, who have suffered as well. Help me love them in ways they will see and that minister to their hurt. Give me what I do not have, Lord, for I know I am not enough.

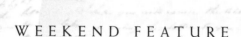

El Roi, God Sees Me

Read Genesis 16:1–14

Tip: Use a journal to respond to the questions in the weekend features. You might want to consider an additional notebook that will allow you space to draw, sketch, or use another form of artistic expression.

Do you ever feel like you've had to shoulder the consequences for other people's rotten decisions?

Abandonment.

Abuse.

Betrayal.

Loss.

The death of your dreams.

This was life for Hagar, where Old Testament slaves lived at the mercy of their owner's choices—good or bad. And Abram and Sarai were responsible for some pretty lousy choices.

God had promised Abram he'd be the father of a great nation, but Abram got tired of waiting for the son who never came along. So instead of trusting God, he impatiently defaulted to the practices of his culture and slept with his wife's maid, Hagar, in order to produce what would be considered a legal heir.

Bad idea. Certainly not God's idea. But this is the sinful nature that runs deep in the DNA we inherited from our first parents, Adam and Eve. It goes something like this: doubt God's character, get impatient, then take matters into our own hands.

The day Hagar fled from Abram's household and hit the streets was probably the worst day of her life. She was a runaway slave with no means of supporting herself or providing for her child. She must have felt desperate, alone, and totally abandoned.

Amazingly, God took on the body of an angel and came looking for her so he could comfort her face-to-face. He cared that much about a despised, pregnant slave girl. He turned her circumstances around and blessed her son, Ishmael.

And God cares that much about you.

Written on Our Hearts

🐾 Describe the moments in your life when you've felt the most desperate and alone. Did you feel abandoned? Abused? Like you were bearing the consequences of other people's horrible decisions? Describe how you felt.

Hagar recognized the unbelievable truth that God cared so much for her that he took on a body to speak with her. God saw her tears, her aching heart, and her thoughts. And he was so moved by her pain that he came to her and transformed her circumstances.

Did Hagar return to Abram's home still a slave? Yes. But with a new relationship with God. And with the promise that God was redeeming her pain for a purpose bigger than anything she could imagine.

Hagar gave God the name *El Roi, the God who sees me.* And she named her son *Ishmael, God hears.* What does it mean to you to know that God sees every detail of your life, including your aching heart, and promises to give even your suffering purpose?

- Imagine that God has come to you personally and is speaking to you about the betrayal and brokenness in your life. What does he see? What words of comfort and promise is he speaking to you?

- God sees you. What do you think he wants you to see about him today? Read the following verses about God as you think about your answer: Isaiah 41:10; Zephaniah 3:17; John 3:16; 1 John 3:1.

Create an object that will remind you that God sees you and place it where you can see it every day. Here are some ideas:
- Paint the words *El Roi* or *God Sees Me* on a rock or piece of wood, or in a frame.
- Paint the words *El Roi* or *God Sees Me* on a baseball cap or hat and wear it.
- Buy a unique pair of glasses and hang them from a lampshade or the rearview mirror of your car to remind you that God sees you.

El Roi is not a Peeping Tom. He is not a judge peering over our shoulder. He is the God who comes for us when everyone else leaves.

Heart Cry

Help me to see you as my *El Roi*, the God who sees me and who comes for me when everyone else turns their backs. Thank you for never abandoning me. Help me see you for who you really are and trust your heart. Heal me, God, in the deepest places of my hurt and need. Help me believe you see me and you care.

I cradle you in my arms.

My Dear Child,
I, the eternal God,
am your refuge and strength;
and underneath all your pain and sorrow,
my everlasting arms
hold you close to my heart.

—YOUR DEVOTED FATHER
FROM DEUTERONOMY 33:27

Invisible

[Hagar] gave this name to the LORD who spoke to her:
"You are the God who sees me," for she said, "I have now
seen the One who sees me."

GENESIS 16:13

It's hard for me to let people see the real me, God. It's too risky. People tend to judge and give easy answers for things they don't know anything about.

And how could anyone understand my crazy life—the compulsions, the voices, the sleeplessness and depression? Who could possibly understand how much I long to please you—but that my longing is overshadowed by guilt for failing to be the person I want to be?

So I hide my desperation. I talk about superficialities. I smile in silence. I tell truth I can hide behind. I let the phone go unanswered and just text when my voice will betray me.

I've mastered the art of invisibility. People look straight through me as if I were a living ghost.

But deep down, I'm lonely and afraid—a child cowering in a dark corner, praying it's safe to come out, to be seen, to be known—truly known in all my messiness and imperfection.

So many people hurt me, God. A thousand times a day I tell myself my world can never be safe again and that it will never be safe to come out of hiding. But more than anything, I long to be seen and known—as ruined and as broken as I am—and to be loved without having to work to fix myself first.

So here I am, Lord, tucked away in a dark corner, peeking through my fingers as I pray, and hoping that you really see me.

My Child,

I see you, but more than that, I *know* you. I know the number of corpuscles that flow through your veins and when your next eyelash will fall to your cheek. I number the beats of your heart and calibrate the electrical impulses of your brain. I knew you before you drew your first breath, and I know when you will breathe your last.

I know your every thought and fear, dear one. I know your past, present, and future. Your heartaches, joys, and sorrows move my heart. Every day I intervene in your life in an infinite number of ways that you never see.

Look at how I loved my daughter Hagar. She was abused and treated ruthlessly as a slave. Her mistress Sarai hated her because she conceived the son Sarai longed to have. It was Sarai's idea to have Hagar sleep with Abram. It wasn't Hagar's fault she became pregnant, but Sarai became jealous and then banished Hagar to the desert to die with her baby.

Hagar—a pregnant slave—was so important to me that I met her face-to-face in the desert. There she named me *El Roi*, "the God who sees me."

I see you, my child. Right here, right now, I am with you. I reached into the darkness of this world to draw you to me, where you find true and lasting safety.

I promise healing for your hurt.

I promise beauty for your ruins.

And I offer true invisibility—your sins erased through Jesus' blood and your insufficiencies swallowed in his grace.

Because I love you.

Hope on the Edge

What things about yourself do you try to hide from others? In what ways do you identify with Hagar's feelings of abandonment?

God not only sees you, he comes for you wherever you are and identifies with you in your pain. Describe what it would feel like for God to meet you in a desert place in your life and pull you into his arms.

Heart Cry

Dear God, give me courage to trust you enough to step out of the shadows and into the light, even when my feelings tell me to play it safe and to hide. Help me trust in you, not imperfect people, as my safety. Most of all, help me trust your heart of love for me more and more each day as my shelter and refuge and my strong tower. Thank you for being my *El Roi*, the God who sees me.

When the Sun Goes Dark

The righteous cry out, and the LORD hears them;
he delivers them from all their troubles.
The LORD is close to the brokenhearted
and saves those who are crushed in spirit.

PSALM 34:17–18

Dear God,

The world went dark the day my child died.

In one second, one phrase, my world went dark. Life became a minefield of memories that remind me my daughter will never be with us again . . . that she chose to take her own life.

I haven't been able to speak those words out loud, Lord. Saying them somehow makes them truer, and I want so very much to believe I could have said something . . . not said something . . . done something to make that day turn out differently. But I didn't, and I'm drowning in guilt. My feelings are a tangle of anger and grief and pain and numbness knotted so tightly, I'm sometimes sure I'm suffocating.

Everything has changed. Doors remain unopened, messages unerased. I no longer take that exit or visit that restaurant. The sound of my ringing phone reminds me her voice has been silenced. Every thought of her is painful. Every thought that excludes her feels like a betrayal. Every memory is a reminder that she chose death over us.

What did I miss? Why didn't I know her suffering was pushing her to this irreversible leap of desperation?

Will healing ever come, Lord, for pain this deep and unrelenting? Hold me, Lord, and help me remember what hope feels like in the dark.

My Dearest Child,

Your heart has endured the most wrenching grief of all—the loss of a child—and the pain is tearing you apart. I hear every accusation you hurl at me, every question regarding my character, and every doubt regarding my love. I know that to you I can appear to be unfair, distant, and cold—a God who stood by while your prayers went unanswered.

Why didn't I stop it? Why didn't I step in?

The only answer to your "whys" is the "Who" behind existence itself. I am your Father God, who loves you. Who loves your daughter. Who has not abandoned you or her to despair or futility.

Your questions and rage are safe with me, my child. I am not offended. I will not walk away or turn my back. I meet you at your greatest point of pain and need, and in that place you will find my grace sufficient and made perfect in your weakness.

Rage. Question. Talk to me. Cry out. I hear even your unspoken words.

I promise to be with you and to bring hope in the morning.

Hope on the Edge

In what ways have you struggled with guilt? How have you addressed those feelings? Where are you now on that journey?

If you are not familiar with the ministry of GriefShare, check their website for resources and for groups in your local community. You can find GriefShare listed in appendix 3.

Heart Cry

Father, this desert of grief feels lonely and futile, but I choose to trust that you weave purpose into all things for your children. Minister comfort to this deep, deep pain. Help me remember not to measure your love by my sight. Give me courage and strength for this journey. Give me wisdom to remember true things and not become stuck in bitterness. Give me rest for the weariness of grieving and hope that rests in trusting who you are in all things—even this.

No More Strength

He gives strength to the weary
and increases the power of the weak.
ISAIAH 40:29

This thing called life has taken a toll on me, God.

I'm beyond exhausted. Weary, bone tired. And I don't feel like I can take another step. Everywhere I turn, life pounds away at me, and I'm panicking. With each passing day, I'm less able to pull myself together.

I long for calm and quiet. I struggle to remember what peace felt like. I try to shut out the chaos in my head and listen for your voice . . . but exhaustion tells me to give up . . . it's too much work. You seem so far away, and I just can't seem to hear you.

It scares me, Lord, when I feel myself reaching for temporary fixes and old crutches. My thoughts scream at me of my failures, as the jury in my mind once again pronounces its verdict that I'm "not worth it" and a loser.

I don't want to listen to lies, Lord, but I'm exhausted.

Betrayal, disappointment, and longing have stolen my strength. I'm tired, God. Tired of feeling like I don't belong anywhere . . . tired of feeling that somehow you made a mistake allowing me to be born in the first place . . . tired of feeling that making the effort is hopeless anyway.

I've been running for far too long, and today, Lord, I'm running out of strength.

Dear Child,

I feel the sting of sweat when it streams into your eyes. I know the ache of illness, the burn of disappointment, and the exhaustion that suffocates sleep from your spirit. I know the pounding of your heart when you cannot catch your breath on a sultry day. I know the weight of weariness that bows your back and saps your spirit.

I know because I took on flesh and blood, sweat and sorrow, betrayal and bruises to sit beside you in the dirt and the darkness— even when you did not see my face or my tears for you. I know because I exchanged my strength for your weariness.

This thing called *life* has taken a toll on you, my child. It took a toll on my Son, who confined himself to a broken human body for you and bound himself to the earth he helped speak into existence.

He chose the bone-crushing, soul-searing, life-killing weariness of this world as he carried your pain upon his shoulders. In him, the past and the present and the future collided in an explosion of victory that forever freed you from the curse of weariness, thirst, and hunger.

This world took a toll upon me, as my beloved Son was torn from my presence on the cross. I expended the riches of my resources out of love for you, my child. Even your exhaustion is meant to draw you to me.

Come to me and find power for your weakness and rest in my love.

Hope on the Edge
How has the pain of life exhausted your body, soul, and spirit? How has God revived your spirit?

How have you found sufficiency in God in your weakness and need?

Heart Cry

God, I trust you to use even weariness and exhaustion for good in my life. My exhaustion makes me dependent, and I will use that dependency to turn to you in ways that will make me more like you. I will listen for your Spirit and turn to your Word and your people as I choose to praise you. Teach me to lean on you as I find rest in who you are.

Hiding the Hurt

You have searched me, LORD,
and you know me.
You know when I sit and when I rise;
you perceive my thoughts from afar. . . .
You are familiar with all my ways.
Before a word is on my tongue
you, LORD, know it completely.
PSALM 139:1–4

Every day it gets harder to put on the show and make it look like I'm okay, God. But I'm not, and you know it.

Once again, I tell myself I *can* do this. I'm *good* at this. That I just have to "disconnect" to get through another hour of the day. Zone out. Float on the surface. Professionals call it *dissociation*. I call it *survival*.

Just put on the mask and nobody will ever see what's going on inside.

But I'm so tired of pretending, Lord. I've got to tell you the truth— so many things are just not right in my life, and I know I don't have the answers. I know I need you.

I hate living in emotional quicksand, and I feel myself sinking deeper every day. I feel the familiar pull of despair that draws my heart further and further from human touch. Even the people closest to me don't see how afraid I am inside. And why should they? I'm a master of disguise. I need to be. How could other people possibly accept the things I've hidden all these years?

But you? You see it *all*—the messes I've tried so hard to sweep under the rug. The secrets that haunt me in the night. The memories I've worked so hard to erase. The shame that stalks me in the shadows.

How could *you* accept the mess of me? Could your love possibly be enough for someone as broken as me?

My Child,

You call yourself "a mess." But what you feel about yourself and what I feel for you are as opposite as the east is from the west.

I see every single tear that has stained your cheeks. Every ache that has torn your heart. When you're overwhelmed, I hear your unspoken prayers. When you're crushed, I hear your pleas for hope. And in those moments, I am moving in your life in a thousand unseen ways.

I created you because my heart desired the precious bond of love that exists between a father and his child that creates a sense of safety and protection—no pretending, no pretense. I know your struggles and failings, but it is impossible for me to see you as a failure. And I know that because of your many wounds, it may be hard for you to trust me. I understand these deep fears.

I am the complete expression of love, and I desire nothing more than to lavish my love on you as your Father. Every good and perfect gift comes from my hand. I love you with an everlasting love, and my thoughts toward you are as countless as the sand on the seashore. I will never stop doing good to you, for you are my cherished possession, and I carry you close to my heart.

I have searched you and known you and all your ways. Nothing can ever separate you from my love.

Hope on the Edge

What "messes" have you tried to hide? God says it's impossible for him to see you as a failure. What is he saying to you now?

In what ways have you been tricked into believing the lie that you're not "good enough" for God to approve of you? See Romans 8:38–39. What does it mean to you that nothing can separate you from God's love?

Heart Cry

Dear God, I need you more than ever before, and I want to stop living behind a mask. Help me see myself the way you see me and grow confident of your approval and secure in your love. May I learn to love and trust you more today than I did yesterday. Open my eyes, Lord, and let me be blown away by the fact that your love for me is infinite and you could never love me more.

Living in the Empty

Out of his fullness we have all received grace in place of grace already given.

JOHN 1:16

It shouldn't be this hard to move, God. But I'm struggling to think the next thought, to take the next step, or to feel anything beyond numb. Please tell me everything will be okay, because right now nothing feels okay. I've hurt for so long, that I've drifted into the only place that seems safe—a numb void where I can't feel the pain. But what I want most of all is to rest my head on your shoulder, bury my face in your neck, and breathe in *you*.

A cold emptiness has settled into my spirit, and it scares me. How is it possible I have you living in my heart, yet I feel barren and forsaken? I know you say you love me, and I believe it in my head. Yet I struggle to feel it . . . why? Why can't I feel your love like other people, God? Am I doing something wrong? Am I too broken?

Sometimes this empty feeling pushes me toward desperation. I feel as if I should be able to fix this part of me and get it right, but I'm not even sure what *it* is. And the longer I'm stuck here, the stronger the despair grows, like a volcano about to erupt.

Lord, please be patient with me. Teach me to trust your heart for me in this dark place. Teach me how to lean on your understanding, because mine is so weak and fragile. Please keep me from giving up when the emptiness feels as if it's pulling me into a bottomless pit. Remind me that hope comes in the morning, and you are the God of the sunrise.

Dear Child,

Your "emptiness" is a longing for me—your soul's deep awareness and quiet confidence that I am here and listening. Although you say you cannot feel me, your soul knows I am here.

Nothing brings me greater joy than your desire to seek me. Some people's interest in me is sustained by emotion. They come to me when feelings stir them, but you labor through the desert out of commitment. No wonder my heart sings over you. Seek me, and you will discover me everywhere as I increase your awareness of my presence.

All you hope for has been fulfilled in Jesus and is working its way to completion. While emotions are one of my gifts to you, they are not the full measure of truth. Emotions can become distorted by pain, be used to validate selfishness, or become idols that keep you from me.

You experienced deep, scarring pain. I built your body, soul, and spirit with intricate mechanisms to protect you so your wounds would not overwhelm and destroy you. The things that often make you feel damaged and different are part of your journey to wholeness and healing.

In those moments when you long to feel my presence, talk to me, my child. Then look for the love I pour out through my Word, nature, the actions of loved ones, and the stirrings of my Spirit.

My limitless grace is yours, and nothing can separate you from my love.

Hope on the Edge

How have emotions worked for you in positive, truthful ways? How have they worked against you in negative ways?

Consider seeking the assistance of a Christian therapist to help you sort through your emotions and the devastation of your trauma. For resources, consult appendix 3 at the back of the book.

Heart Cry

Dear Father, thank you that my feelings don't define me or who you call me to be. Thank you for grace that binds me to your love in all things. Give me the wisdom to believe your truth trumps my feelings. Give me love that walks through the desert for the simple joy of knowing you more.

Blessing Our Children

Read Matthew 18:21–35

People who suffer from PTSD have often been victims of abuse, violence, betrayal, horror, and injustice. As a result, they often carry anger at God and at the people who hurt them. They sometimes harbor bitterness, develop a victim mentality, and live in cycles of reactive living that block them from healing.

We all pass down attitudes within our family culture for future generations. I harbored bitterness, anger, and a victim mentality after I was attacked by a serial rapist. I hung onto my hatred for years before I admitted that my attitudes were poisoning my life and my children.

Forgiveness isn't a "free pass" for people who have wronged us. It doesn't free them from consequences; it frees us. The Bible states that God forgives us with the same measure of forgiveness we grant to others (Matthew 6:14–15). We can't say we love God if we don't love people—even the most imperfect.

Written on Our Hearts
God's Word has a lot to say about forgiving enemies and those who persecute us.

🐦 Look back at your family. Have the actions of past generations hurt you? In what ways? How have you dealt with that pain?

🐦 In what ways were those who hurt you themselves hurt by family members, strangers, or life circumstances? How did their trauma shape them?

🐦 In what ways has Satan been successful in creating a heritage of betrayal, shame, abuse, wounding, and pain in your family?

Our culture tells us to pay back hurt with hurt. God's Word tells us to forgive as God forgave us.

🐦 In what ways would forgiveness on the part of parents, grandparents, aunts, uncles, other relatives, or friends have reshaped your life? How could your forgiveness reshape future generations?

🐦 Spend time in prayer over the next few days. In what ways is God calling you to create a new heritage of blessing for future generations in your family? What would it look like for you to take positive steps to cancel out anger, blame, unforgiveness, a victim mentality, and other destructive attitudes? Ask the Spirit of God to show you areas where he would like to grow you more into the likeness of Jesus. Pray through these verses as you think about your answers: Matthew 5:21–24; 2 Corinthians 5:18–19; Matthew 6:14–15; 18:21–35.

❧ Write a letter of blessing to future generations. In what ways do you commit, through the power of God, to break the cycle of pain in your family and create a new heritage of blessing in your attitudes, spiritual life, and conduct as a gift to future generations?

Heart Cry

Lord God, today I claim new territory of healing and freedom not just for me but also for my family. I need you now more than ever as I walk this new path and choose new ways of thinking. Help me trust you and you alone and claim your promises for my life.

WEEK THREE

I comfort you.

*I will sustain you
according to my promise,
and you will live;
because of me, your hope
will not be dashed.*

—YOUR FATHER GOD
FROM PSALM 119:116

Things That Go Bump
in the Night

My soul yearns for you in the night;
in the morning my spirit longs for you.
When your judgments come upon the earth,
the people of the world learn righteousness.

ISAIAH 26:9

I tuck my iPod beneath my pillow, God, and pray that the music will drive the monsters into the shadows. That as my head touches sheets scented with another night's hope, flashbacks will not flood my body—sensations that suffocate awareness of the present from my mind. That I'll not be slammed into terrorizing darkness and fear.

When that happens, I gasp for air as I fight the predator who's invaded my mind yet again. We battle. He wins. When I finally sleep, he stalks me again into the shadows, and I awake, screaming. I do not know how much time has passed. I only know that night after night I am living prey and eaten alive.

Every night I lie awake in terror, God.

Afraid of the dark.

Afraid to move.

Afraid of the silence.

Afraid of noise.

Afraid of my breathing.

Afraid that each breath will be my last.

The child inside me screams out to hide under the bed, but I know that monsters will come for me even there. They came for me as a child when I was raped in a church basement, and they stalk me when I cross the threshold and pass through a church door.

I've heard pastors say that Christians are God's soldiers. But how can I be a soldier if I'm afraid of the dark? And if I hate your house of worship?

Mostly, I'm afraid I'm a failure, afraid that I'm stuck in this place, living forever in a nightmare.

Dear One,

You have relentlessly attacked the Enemy on the battlefield of your mind with every resource within your reach. Your eyes do not see the blows you have successfully landed and the victories you have won. Each time you turn to me in faith, the Enemy of your soul falls screaming to his knees. He is a defeated foe and cowers before you, my daughter.

My Spirit goes before you, fending the blows that Satan aims to sever the lifeblood of truth that flows through your veins. In battle after battle, you have come to me in spite of struggles, doubts, and questions. The Enemy fears your power and recoils in your presence.

You are wise to reach for music as David did to fortify his soul. Music is a weapon that unleashes heavenly power. Be strengthened by the power of my Word. Know that your story has already been rewritten and your healing secured through Jesus.

Among Jesus' disciples and closest companions was a physician.

The apostle Paul chose a doctor to accompany him to prison in his time of greatest need. Seek my healing gifts through doctors and the gifts of those who can lead you into health.

You are victorious through the blood of Jesus. I sing over you with joy for your strength and faithfulness in the battle.

Hope on the Edge

Have you struggled with nightmares or flashbacks? They are symptoms of trauma and PTSD and can be treated. Talk to a traumatologist who understands the methods that can be implemented. Consult appendix 3 for possible resources.

What tools have you used to combat nightmares and flashbacks? What has helped you? Envision Jesus meeting you in those dreams with a new ending. Write them out, then read them aloud.

Heart Cry

Dear God, give me the courage to move out of this place of despair and to walk toward healing and hope. Direct me to people who understand how to fight trauma and PTSD. Help me release the judgment that often comes from those who don't understand my illness and how I feel. Help me see myself as a warrior and keep turning to you in the battle.

Falling Apart

I'll never forget the trouble, the utter lostness,
the taste of ashes, the poison I've swallowed.
I remember it all—oh, how well I remember—
the feeling of hitting the bottom.
But there's one other thing I remember,
and remembering, I keep a grip on hope:
GOD's loyal love couldn't have run out,
his merciful love couldn't have dried up.
They're created new every morning.
How great your faithfulness!
I'm sticking with GOD (I say it over and over).
He's all I've got left.
GOD proves to be good to the man who passionately waits,
to the woman who diligently seeks.
It's a good thing to quietly hope,
quietly hope for help from GOD.
LAMENTATIONS 3:19–26 MSG

I'm falling apart, God. Emptiness has snuffed out the hope that convinces me to take the next breath. Life has spun out of control, and it's taken me with it. I thought if I just locked away certain thoughts and focused on one moment—one second—at a time, I could make it through the next day. But every day has gotten harder, and there just aren't enough chances to come up for air anymore.

I'm scared and don't know what to do. I don't know where to turn, and my fears keep me from trusting the people I used to run to. I don't think I have what it takes to survive this, Lord. I want to do the right thing . . . but I'm not sure what the right thing is anymore.

Doubt tells me I can't trust you, I can't trust my friends, and I certainly can't trust myself. I want to trust you as the *only one* who can ever fill the hole inside me . . . but I'm afraid of one more disappointment.

I hate this place where I only hear the sound of my own condemning voice. I need to hear you, God.

Please hold me together and save me from this despair.

Dearest Child,

The Enemy attacks you because you are mine. He desires to make you doubt my love and my character. He has cast you into a dungeon of despair, but even there, I never leave you or forsake you.

You believe your pain is void of purpose. You look at your past and see a ravaged life. You look at today and see chaos. You look at tomorrow and see hopelessness as you grope for answers.

How long? Why?

My child, you ask the wrong questions. The better question is, "Given the darkness in the world and in me, what can I learn?"

In the dungeon of your soul you discover your need of me and your hidden desires to destroy those who hurt you.

Let darkness drive you to a deeper awareness of your need for me. Let it drive you to discover hidden agendas, secret motives, and self-justified hatred. Your longing for answers and justice can never be satisfied. These things, my child, bring the damnation of everyone in this sinful world, apart from my love.

Lay down your preconceived notions of who I am and learn of me as my Spirit moves in you. When you feel you are falling apart, you will find my unfailing love to be the certainty upon which you can rest. But my child, be wise and seek physicians who can provide physical answers for the unity of your body, soul, and spirit.

Seek me and you will find me. Keep your grip on hope. My merciful love never runs out, and I am making all things new again.

Hope on the Edge

What does it mean for you to reach out and find help and to trust God for something new? Ask him to bring you a reliable friend and to show you new opportunities for healing.

How does God speak to you in the moments when you feel like you're falling apart?

Heart Cry

Dear God, escaping is a fairy tale because I always take myself with me. I know I need to stop running and find help. Show me who to turn to and who to talk to. Help me to give up my made-up ideas about who you are, and help me to learn who you really are and to trust you, no matter what. Give me new hope and strengthen my faith.

The Movie Screen of My Mind

My sacrifice, O God, is a broken spirit;
a broken and contrite heart
you, God, will not despise.

PSALM 51:17

The house is silent and still as candlelight dances on the living-room walls. But the peaceful mood doesn't match what's happening inside of me, God. I can't quiet the noise inside my head as scene after scene plays through my memory.

Bad choices flash through my mind like a 3-D movie. Once again I'm stuck in a familiar scene of regret and shame. God, I'm scared I won't be able to hear your voice over the voices in my head reminding me what I've done, telling me it's all my fault, branding me as a failure. I'm afraid I'll never get the memories out of my head and that I can never be free of the past.

I'm taunted with images that flood me with shame, and I cower in the darkness with my hands over my face. I feel helpless against the weight of regret that crushes me. I struggle to remember who I am and who I'm not, but the mire of my past pulls me more deeply into the pit.

Memory flings demeaning words across time, and they find an easy grip on my heart. I've tried to erase the pictures and words, but they invade the cracks and spaces of my mind. I've filled those spaces with other things—distractions, activities, good things and bad. I've grabbed at anything that would help me forget.

But here I am again. I can't outrun my past, I can't run from you, and I can't hide from myself.

My past does not define me, God. I know that truth in my head. Help me believe it in my heart.

The things you regret are ghosts of the past that were crucified and buried in Jesus' tomb more than two thousand years ago. His resurrection placed a grave marker on your sins and failures.

I have forgiven you of every wrong, uncaring, inappropriate, miscalculated, or outright evil deed you ever committed. I have forgiven you of things you do not even know to regret because you are still growing in discernment. Your sins—past, present, and future—are covered by the blood of Jesus, and I remember them no more. When he died, he erased the guilt of your past and any relationship to sin. The regret that taunts you is Satan's attempt to delude you into thinking you are still defeated, worthless, and trapped by these things. Nothing could be a bigger lie.

When images of regret flash through your mind, envision Jesus on the cross, looking down at you and saying, "It is finished. You are free." When the thud of accusatory words hits your heart, picture Jesus looking at you from the cross and whispering words of love. When shame floods your heart, feel his loving arms around you, enfolding you in his embrace.

Satan wants to rob you of your future and your hope by keeping you bound to the past. But, my child, you cannot be condemned for what no longer exists. Jesus invaded time to redeem your past, your present, and your future. He bought it and paid for it and offers you freedom, hope, and a future in its place.

Claim these things because they are yours. Envision my dreams and hopes for you as you cling to your true identity as my child—forgiven and free.

Hope on the Edge
How has Satan used your past to strip you of hope and a future? What is God's perspective on these things?

What would it mean to you to have someone pay off your biggest debt? In what ways would that free you? Now imagine that everything you've ever regretted or been ashamed of has been paid for and erased. In what ways does that free you?

Heart Cry
Dear Father, Jesus paid for my past, present, and future with his blood, and I am free. Sometimes it's hard for me to feel like this is true, but I won't cheapen his sacrifice with my guilt. Help me believe and walk in the truth that I am beloved, chosen, and your child. Thank you that I can live free from regret and filled with gratitude for my future.

The Ragged Edge of Hopelessness

Be alert and of sober mind. Your enemy the devil prowls around like a roaring lion looking for someone to devour.

1 PETER 5:8

God, the battle of my life is raging. It feels like I'm on the losing side, and I'll only lose this battle once.

I'm struggling to make it to the end of the day, and nobody knows it. Staying alive has become my full-time job, and I feel like the time has come to clock out.

I tell myself I'm not needed anymore. Other people can do the things I've been doing. My family members are loved and cared for. Sure, they'll grieve, but I'm drowning in this ocean of darkness. Struggles have come in waves over the years, but they're coming harder and faster, and I can feel myself being pulled under. I've grown weary, Lord, and you're my only hope.

But the nights drag on forever, God. I fight the lies that tell me I'm not worth it, that the world is better off without me, that it will always be like this. But it's hard for me to see past the pain. I'm living on the ragged edge of that place called hopelessness.

And I'm scared.

I don't want to die, and I don't want to hate living. I want to know what hope feels like again.

Dear God, please rescue me from this dark place. If I ever needed you, dear Father, it's now.

Dear Child,

Rescue begins when you reach out and grasp the hands of those I have sent—family, friends, those in the body of Christ around you. The Enemy has seduced you into retreating into a place of hiding, secrecy, and silence. He has deceived you into thinking that your life has no purpose—that the best is behind you, that you have no more to offer, that the pain is too great to go on.

Satan is a liar and a thief from the beginning. Because he knows your true power, his goal is to destroy you and all my children and to crush all things I call good. But I call you to life, my child. I call you to healing. I call you to hope. And I call you to a purpose that will echo through the generations and into eternity.

I also understand that pain, suffering, abandonment, betrayal, and exhaustion have stripped you of hope. Look around you, child. Look for my love in the faces of those you have shut out. Look for my resources behind doors you have closed. Look for hope down paths you have rejected. I have not abandoned you. I am at work around you. Look for me.

I am speaking to you. Rescue is here. It is now. My hand is extended to you in love.

Hope on the Edge

Suicidal thoughts can be a symptom of trauma and PTSD. God does not judge depression and despair as sin. He is with us in the darkest moments of our lives, and he does not leave us alone. Who would

God want you to talk to about feelings of depression or despair if you were feeling suicidal? Make a plan for accountability, should depression take you to a level of self-harm.

Satan's intention is to "devour" us in despair, doubt, and discouragement. What steps can you take to engage in warfare against suicidal urges on a spiritual level? And what steps can you take practically to protect yourself and your loved ones?

Heart Cry

Dear God, thank you for loving me unrelentingly. I renounce any connections that have bound me to Satan in my past and given him power over me, and I take back authority over my life as your child. I claim my life and my power as a child of God, redeemed through the blood of Christ. I claim the hope and healing you offer. And I will take steps to tell someone who can help me out of this place of despair.

See appendix 3 for a listing of crisis hotlines and treatment options.

Here I Am Again

For God did not send his Son into the world to condemn the world, but to save the world through him.
JOHN 3:17

I'm lost in the desert and walking in circles, Lord. Guilt sweeps over my footprints like a sandstorm, and when the storm has cleared and I open my eyes, I'm always back where I began.

For years I've believed that something new—something better—was over the next hill and that if I just kept on trudging, I could get past my past. That I could show up when and where I'm supposed to show up. Do the things people expect me to do. Do the things I want so much to do for you, God. But lately I can't pick up my feet. I'm too exhausted to move any further in this desert of rocks and stones.

The whispers in my head have turned to shouts, and the words are far from kind. I'm tired of the struggle, and I can read people's unspoken thoughts.

When is she going to get over it? She's been doing this same old stuff for years. Other people move on past the rough spots in life; why not her?

I see the judgment in their eyes. They wait. And watch. Expect me to do life better. And sometimes I can . . . for a while.

Then I'm back where I started, and the critical chatter in my head begins again, and the journey begins again. The same endless path to nowhere.

Fear. Paralysis. Guilt. Self-loathing. Grabbing for things that dull the pain.

I hate living in this desert of guilt and shame. Show me the way out, God, or I'll be wandering here forever on my own.

My Dear One,

I'm with you in this desert because my love for you isn't based on performance. My love is an eternal, unchanging, immovable force.

I have never expected you to get life "right." Nothing you do can stir me to love you more or diminish my love. My love is never tethered to performance. I love you because you are uniquely you. I love you because you are my idea, my conception, my creation, my joy. I love you because you are my own, my beloved, my child.

When I look at you, I see perfection, limitless possibilities, beauty. I see all that I conceived for you before the creation of the world. I see the same perfection I see when I look at Jesus.

You are *not* tied to your past. Jesus set you free. When you accepted him, a double exchange took place, and your sin became his as his righteousness and identity became yours. You now live empowered and free to accomplish every good thing I have called you to do. Your past is erased.

I have called you to a hope and a future more real than any dream you could imagine. Draw life from knowing who you are in me as your desert blooms into an oasis.

Rest from striving to please me. I love you. Unconditionally. I am with you on the journey, holding your hand, and even this wilderness experience is bringing you to a destination of purpose.

Do not fear when you do not see footprints in the sand leading you to a destination, my child, for I am carrying you, and I know the way.

Hope on the Edge

We often find a need to see our way through the deserts of life. What does it mean to know that God is carrying you and knows the final destination?

What good things is God calling you to do? What dreams and visions has he whispered in your ear?

Heart Cry

Dear Father, I choose to step away from the mirror of self-doubt and self-condemnation and claim my identity in you as I walk into my future one moment at a time. I reject fear and doubt, because I cannot see what lies ahead. I claim glory and beauty and purpose in Jesus' name because I am yours.

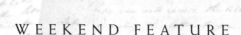

Mending the Memories
Read 2 Corinthians 4:7

The Father's Invitation

Perhaps the idea of knowing Jesus Christ personally is new to you. God came to earth to solve the sin problem that invades every aspect of our world, from creation to the human heart. We sin by birth (our heritage in Adam and Eve) and by choice. Our sin separates us from God, but he made a way for us to be restored to him because of his unfathomable love for us. John 3:16 tell us that God loved the world so much that he sacrificed his own Son so we can be free from the penalty of sin and enjoy an intimate, face-to-face relationship with him.

If you have never asked Jesus to forgive your sins and given your life to him as your Lord and Savior, consider asking him to do that today in a simple prayer. "God, I confess my sins and my need of you. Take my life and change me. I give you my sins and gratefully accept your free gift of forgiveness. Amen."

Making All Things New

The following love letter from God is based on 2 Corinthians 4:7. Take time to meditate on it and reflect on what it means to you personally.

My Precious One,

You are a "jar of clay." You are not perfect, and this comes as no surprise to me. You make mistakes, fail, and sin, and those things spill out into the lives of others and hurt them. And their brokenness, sins, and flaws spill out into your life. You are hurt, and sometimes you feel worthless and beyond repair. Ruined.

But I chose you out of my great love and placed my treasure in you. I gave you the gift of my own perfect Son, whose glory shines through you as my daughter.

You are my treasure. I have blessings stored up for you, and as you come to understand who you are, you will also understand what you must do and find the strength I have given you through Jesus and my Holy Spirit.

I love you beyond any words you could understand, my daughter. Your tears are precious to me. I am moved by every hurt and pain that you feel. But as the sovereign God of the universe, I am weaving everything that touches you into a tapestry of beauty that you will one day see with eyes of understanding.

I have heard your cries and cried with you. I have seen every single tear and kept track of each one. And I can tell you with the love of a perfect Father, that even though things may seem pointless at this moment, I am making all things right for you, beyond anything you can think or imagine.

Love,
Your Father God

Written on Our Hearts

"The LORD has heard my weeping. The LORD has heard my cry for mercy." —Psalm 6:8–9

- What is your greatest source of tears? Imagine that Jesus has invited you to sit at his feet. Tell him about your wounds. He's listening and longs to have you share your heart.

- What do these Scriptures—Psalms 3:3; 28:7; 56:8—tell you about God's heart for you?

Heart Cry

Father, help me to see your heart for me and to run to you like a child who trusts her father. Help me overcome my fears and learn to love you more as I lay down my misconceptions and see love that never gives up on me.

WEEK FOUR

I remember you.

*Be strong,
and let your heart take courage,
because I wait for you.*
—YOUR FATHER GOD
FROM PSALM 31:24

Standing at the Window

Even though I walk
through the darkest valley,
I will fear no evil,
for you are with me.
PSALM 23:4

Dear God,

Even though I'm an adult, part of me still feels like an abandoned child. People betrayed me, didn't show up, and left me standing at the window. Part of me is still that child, standing alone and afraid, waiting to see headlights come back up the driveway.

I'm angry at myself for my fears, but day after day I'm capital A-F-R-A-I-D. I've tried to break away from this spot where my soul is chained, but I always end up back in the same place.

So I protect myself. I walk away first. I refuse to allow people over the wall to get near me. Or I fight the urge to cling so tightly that I'm afraid to ever let go. I want to *know* the people I love are coming back . . . that they haven't forgotten me. But life doesn't come with guarantees.

God, I want to believe you won't turn your back on me. I don't want to live with this fear and uncertainty forever. Will the feeling in the pit of my stomach ever go away? How can I know you'll be with me *forever* and that you won't give up on me?

Do you know I'm afraid? Do you really know *me*? Please don't forget me. I've tried to be strong and handle the betrayal. I can handle almost anything.

Except to be forgotten.

So I've come to you today, asking you to take away this fear.

Asking you not to give up on me.

My Precious Child,

I never abandoned you, although you often felt that way. Pain has a way of making me invisible to my children. But the deep places of your heart know I am here, and you come to me.

I see your tears and number them. I know their taste as they brush your lips. I feel every sob, and I weep with you. Everything I do is rooted and hemmed in by love for you. It is impossible for me to act apart from love.

What you felt then and feel now is pain produced by the sinful choices of broken people. As you walk through life, what you see are the chaotic fragments of this world.

What you don't see is the work I am doing in the chaos because of my great love for you.

Then and now and before you were born, I was at work and am at work, protecting you from the full weight of the curse sin is hurling at you and those you love.

Shielding your soul from the crushing blows Satan intended to use to decimate you that day and every day.

Securing loving family and friends to search for you, to find you, to comfort you, to show you the face of Jesus.

Your name is inscribed on my hands. My love for you is written in the heavens. I sacrificed my own Son because of my love for you. The history of the world is being written because of my love for you.

I am always beside you. I will *never* leave you or forsake you. And I will never tire of speaking those words to you.

Hope on the Edge
How has abandonment influenced your story? How has God challenged you to grow in spite of your fears?

How has God shown up for you in times when you've felt abandoned? What did those moments look like?

Heart Cry
Dear Father, your love never fails, and your mercies are new every morning. Thank you for never getting frustrated with me. Help me lean into you as my ultimate source of hope and renew my thoughts as I focus on your unmoving, unshakable love for me.

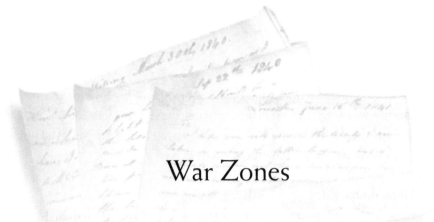

War Zones

When the angel of the LORD appeared to Gideon, he said, "The
LORD is with you, mighty warrior."
JUDGES 6:12

Nothing could have prepared me to walk through this battle zone, God. No field exercise could have simulated the shock of losing a buddy who was standing next to me and in the blink of an eye was gone forever. Nothing could have trained me to steel myself for carnage and the irrevocable reality of death.

You didn't create us to ravage one another, Lord, but we do, and your earth is a war zone of walking wounded.

Part of me came home from battle. The other part was taken captive, and I feel as if I'll never be free. Missiles scream through my head every day, but I'm the only one who hears them. Unseen enemies lurk in every shadow, and my eyes are never at rest as I search for signs of movement. Unseen enemies threaten me from every shadow and around every corner. The hypervigilance that served me in battle has become my enemy at home. The adrenaline rush that kept me alive has become a destructive addiction. The need to stuff my feelings and move on that helped me fulfill the next mission is killing me now.

I'm frozen, and I don't know how to move forward, Lord.

The pain is coming out in rage. I'm hurting myself and the people I love, and I don't know how to stop.

I've brought the war home with me, but I'm ready to surrender.

You paid an immeasurable price to sacrifice your welfare on behalf of others, my mighty warrior-child. Battle always comes at a cost, and you paid dearly. So few know the terrors of the unseen war within. But your sacrifice has not gone unnoticed and will not go unrewarded.

You have been a good and faithful soldier. You volunteered for the battle, in spite of the cost. You were faithful to your call. You fought well, and you finished the fight, in spite of the visible and invisible wounds you bore.

Now it is time to pursue healing. It is time to lay down the strategies of war and seek the blessings of restoration. Admit you need help. Lean on the resources of those around you. Grant them grace, for they do not understand the conflict you face day and night. Engage in whatever strategies are best for you to find physical, mental, and emotional healing. I give good gifts, my child, and at times you are responsible for seeking them out in order to put them to use.

Surrender your need. Seek healing. Know that you are fully known, unconditionally loved, and forever blessed.

I am with you, my warrior-child, and I grant you courage for this battle, weapons for this fight, and new mercies every morning.

Hope on the Edge

How have your war experiences—literal or figurative—changed you and the way you cope with life, your responsibilities at home and at work, and your relationships? What resources have you found to help you heal and move forward?

If you're a veteran, consider connecting with PTSDPerspectives .org for resources on post-traumatic stress disorder. You can find other resources listed in appendix 3, including the VA PTSD program locator.

Heart Cry

God, it's hard to admit I need help, but I do. The survival skills that served me in war are destroying me at home. Give me courage to talk about the war inside me and to go for help. Take care of my family, and help me learn how to love them the way I long to love them. Please take my wounds and use them to glorify you.

God of Dark Places

Then Jesus came with them to a place called Gethsemane, and
said to His disciples, "Sit here while I go over there and pray."
And He took with Him Peter and the two sons of Zebedee, and
began to be grieved and distressed. Then He said to them,
"My soul is deeply grieved, to the point of death; remain here
and keep watch with Me."

MATTHEW 26:36–38 NASB

Nobody wants to say this out loud, Lord, but I believe Jesus was depressed. Isaiah 53:3 says he was "despised and rejected by mankind, a man of suffering and familiar with pain."

A God who wrestled with grief and sorrow is a God I can hang onto. Depression doesn't mean people are wimps. Jesus was perfect, right? He was the holy God who willingly put himself into a sweaty body so he could be crushed by the degradation of rape, incest, child abuse, domestic violence, and every perversion and sin man ever devised.

Jesus was not God who fell into sin, but God who absorbed the weight of our sin. He became fully human—even in his emotions. So I have to believe he struggled with depression.

A lot of people—especially Christians—make depression unholy and sinful. They make it a cake-mix problem with a just-add-verses solution. The Jesus I see in the garden of Gethsemane the night before he was crucified knew you more intimately than anyone. He not only knew your Word, he was your living Word. Yet he struggled.

He was grieved, distressed, and in a fragile state of mind. He went to his disciples and asked them to stick it out with him through the night. He asked you to release him from his suffering. He suffered in mental torment. This was as real as suffering with depression gets.

And still, Jesus didn't sin.

God, I just want to say thank you for loving us enough to send your Son to truly to walk through this world to experience my pain. Then to overcome the sin and suffering of this world so we could have hope.

Jesus felt the full weight of his sacrifice begin to fall with crushing weight as he prayed in the garden of Gethsemane. He knew the indescribable suffering he would face as he bore the sins of all humanity. But the greatest heartbreak he faced was grappling with the irrefutable truth that I would be forced to turn away from him and abandon him—the Son I dearly loved. He begged me to find another way.

Yes, Jesus felt isolated and alone. He knew even his closest friends could not possibly understand what he was going through. And even though he begged them to stay with him, they failed him and fell asleep.

My Son pleaded with me in anguish. He was grieved beyond words to the point of physical breakdown. He was both fully God and fully human, yet he submitted to my will and resigned himself to my plan because he trusted me in spite of what he would suffer and because he loved you more than his own life.

Did Jesus experience your every grief and sorrow? Yes. And he did it not just willingly, but embracing the full cost because you were far more valuable than his suffering. When the soldiers offered gall—a drink that would have dulled the pain—Jesus refused it so he could experience the full weight of your suffering. He refused to escape even the slightest bit of your suffering, so you could be free.

Jesus' love for you is so great that no power in heaven or hell could hold him back from giving his life for you by slipping into an earthly body of limitation, frustration, and betrayal, to redeem you through his agonizing death.

Trust the love that moved the universe and broke the chains of hell for you to light your way in the darkest places of your life.

Hope on the Edge

Have you struggled with depression? Depression is often a chemical imbalance in the brain that can be addressed through medication, diet, exercise, and other approaches. Consult your physician or mental health professional if you are struggling with depression.

Depression also has deep spiritual roots and effects. What have you found to be effective in helping you?

Heart Cry

Thank you, Jesus, for loving me so much that you chose to live in a body that could feel my pain. Thank you for loving us in our imperfections and our sufferings. Give me faith to do the things I can do to walk in health and to draw me closer to you.

No More Pretending

Be strong and courageous. Do not be afraid or terrified because of them, for the LORD your God goes with you; he will never leave you nor forsake you.

DEUTERONOMY 31:6

"She certainly kept her feelings hidden. Of all the people to commit suicide, I'd never have thought it would ever be her."

I've heard words like those more than once, Lord, and I've inwardly smiled. Few of my friends and family would ever suspect how many times I've planned my suicide, would know what a relief it would be not to live in the chaos inside my head.

They don't have a clue about the struggles I hide inside. If I could get brownie points in heaven for putting on a show, I'd be a winner. I take care of my family, work hard at my job, volunteer for worthy causes, give to the poor, and dress and talk like a professional.

My best role is professional pretender—hiding the screaming voices, compulsions, and emotions that teeter on the verge of despair day after day. I've envisioned my death in a hundred ways, God. Dreamed about drifting into a black oblivion that would end the struggle I've fought so long to hide.

Day after day the voices inside my head tell me to end my life and stop pretending. Lies and fragments of my past echo through my days and nights.

Then there's your voice, God, reminding me that suicide solves nothing. Reminding me of the people you've entrusted to me. Reminding me there's hope in you. Telling me you're with me and not to give up.

Help me choose life, Lord, not because I'm feeling the way I hope to feel in this moment, but because I choose to live and move in you and not out of my own limited resources.

Breathe life back into these dry bones, Lord, and give me your hope for my despair.

Suicide is the sound of a door slamming with a force so powerful its fragments shatter into countless lives in future generations.

Right now you are overwhelmed by pain so great you find the present unbearable, and you are sinking beneath the weight. Your feelings are time-bound, but my purpose for you surpasses feelings, pain, time, and the temporal things you now see and understand.

I care deeply about your feelings and pain. Your depression is a natural result of what you've been through. But there is healing to be found. I created the laws of science that govern your body and the laws of chemistry that provide tools of remedy for humanity to discover and apply with wisdom. Science belongs to me and is a tool for my children's blessing.

I call you to true life. Do not be defeated by the lie of shame. Speak truth and find wisdom and counsel in those I have placed around you. I want my children to live healthy and whole. Tear down the wall of shame that separates you from me as I draw you to me. I am drawing you to me in love.

The ultimate deception of suicide is that it is a solution. Instead, it sows the seeds of pain and the lie of futility into the lives of those left behind.

I call you to life, my child. Rebuke the lies. Seek healing. Draw close to me.

Hope on the Edge

As women who have suffered trauma live into their forties and fifties with untreated PTSD, their coping mechanisms begin to wear out, and many begin to feel increasingly suicidal. Evaluate how you've coped with your trauma. Is it getting easier? Harder? Have you found good treatment resources and put them to use? Prayerfully consider the treatment options and resources suggested in appendix 3. And if you have never told anyone about your trauma experiences, consider telling as a first step.

If you feel you are in a crisis, please call a suicide prevention hotline. Many have resources for substance abuse, economic concerns, depression, and mental and physical illnesses. The National Suicide Prevention hotline number is 1-800-273-8255.

Heart Cry

Dear God, I hate feeling hopeless. Point me to the doctors, counselors, pastors, and friends who can help me. Give me courage to be honest. Help me reject the shame that comes from others, and to forgive them for their often hurtful and ignorant comments. Help me see myself as you see me, and heal me, Lord.

A Long Way Off

*While he was still a long way off, his father saw him and was
filled with compassion for him; he ran to his son, threw his arms
around him and kissed him.*

LUKE 15:20

Someone once told me if I feel far from you, God, you're not the one
who moved. But other people picked my body up and slammed it
down this dark hole. And from the bottom of a dark hole, it's hard
to believe I can ever make my way back to the light and to you, God.

I keep telling myself I need to do something to earn my way out,
to erase my mistakes, and to pay for my messes. I'm pretty sure you're
ashamed of me and all the things I've done just to survive and to
try to scrub away my pain. I never expected to end up in this place.
Addicts are supposed to be those "other" people. I always thought I
could handle my problems and give up the drugs—that I just needed
them to help me through the rough spaces for a while.

And the cutting and burning? I know I'm not supposed to treat my
body that way. But deep inside I tell myself I have to control something in my crazy life, that I won't need these things forever, even
though it already feels like forever.

So here I am, a long way from you, God. A long way from people
who are standing next to me. A long way from hope. At least that's what
it feels like to me, looking up from the bottom of this deep, dark pit.

But I can still see your face. And I'm calling out to you because I believe you see me here and you're listening. I'm hoping that because you're God, you're really not far away, no matter how I feel.

Dearest Child,

I am your *Abba* Father, your daddy. My plans for you stretch beyond your wildest imagination. And when you turn from me to your own plans, I am always waiting for you to come back. My heart is *for* you, my daughter, and I long for every good thing for you.

I made every preparation to care for you when I created the universe. I set into motion the eternal solution to the ultimate problem of this world—not a short-term solution that gives everyone what they want in life or wipes out the consequences of people's actions. I offer people freedom to choose sin or righteousness, truth or lies. As the ultimate solution to all of life's tangled mess, I offer forgiveness and compassion, grace and mercy through my Son, Jesus. I did this because my heart's longing is for you to know life and hope and joy and goodness and blessing and to know me.

I created you to be in a relationship of trust with me. I alone am trustworthy. My love never changes. I am the same yesterday, today, and forever, and I proved my love for you when I freely gave my own Son to die for you.

This is not a conceptual, theological truth. Jesus' death was a wrenching sacrifice that tore my heart and is an ever-present eternal reality for me. But his death was driven by my love for you.

Because I am your daddy, you can run to me any moment. I am as close as a prayer, as near as a thought, and the force behind your every heartbeat and breath.

In this moment of darkness, know that you are safe because nothing can separate you from my love as I speak life into your soul through the power of my Spirit.

My child, I'm never far away, no matter how you may feel or how hard life may be. I never take my eyes from you or move a footfall from your side. I am not sitting in some distant heaven, looking down on your life. My presence is integral to your very existence. In me you live and move and have your being.

You are never out of my sight. Never out of my care. Never out of my reach. Never too far from grace.

Hope on the Edge

When have you felt the farthest from God? What gave you hope that he was still near, no matter how you felt?

God's love never changes, and he alone is worthy of trust. How have your circumstances made it difficult to believe this? How does believing it influence your life?

Heart Cry

Dear God, help me see you as my Daddy who loves and adores me. Help me trust you to be like a father who cannot rest unless his child is safe at home, who races to me with outstretched arms. Help me trust that kind of relentless love that never fails. And when my trust is tested, help my faith grow stronger.

Abba Father, The God Who Comes Running

Read Luke 15:1–2, 11–32

Have you ever had trouble believing God loves you personally, intimately, and unconditionally? Has your image of God been influenced by men who've hurt you and disappointed you—possibly your own father, stepfather, adoptive father, or foster father who didn't match up to an image of a good and loving father?

Written on Our Hearts

- In what ways have your earthly father's shortcomings and sins influenced your image of God as your father?

- Do you struggle trusting God as someone who loves you unconditionally, protects you, is for you, and never gives up on you?

- Describe your image and view of God. What experiences have shaped this image? Where do those experiences and beliefs line up with or come into conflict with what the Bible teaches about the character of God?

🐟 Has it become easier or harder to trust God over the years? Why do you think this is true?

In the Old Testament, God was known as the Father of the nation of Israel, but his identity as "Father" was a corporate identity to his people. God's relationship as our Father shifts in the New Testament, however, when Jesus refers to him as *Abba*, or *daddy—his* father. Jesus made it clear that he had a father-son relationship with God and gives us a picture of it in the story of the prodigal son in Luke 15:11–32. This is the same personal father-child relationship we have with our Father God, our *Abba* Daddy.

In biblical times, the Middle Eastern father was a patriarch who held power over the family. Cultural etiquette dictated that fathers maintain their dignity. They never ran, which was shameful and put them at risk of exposing their legs in public. Most fathers of that era would have chosen a public ritual of shunning if their wayward child had come home. But the father in the story of the prodigal son stood waiting and watching. He couldn't wait for the moment when he could race to his child, robes flapping and exposing himself to disgrace for the community to see, all for the love of his son.

This is God's love for you—a father racing to you through clouds of dust to wrap you in an embrace of welcome. No matter what you've done. No matter what anyone else thinks. And to honor you with the best that he has and show you off.

Your *Abba*. Your Daddy.

🐟 Think about the worst thing you've ever done. Think about the shame and guilt it caused you. Now think about walking up a long dusty road and looking up and seeing God running toward you with sheer delight that you've come home. Describe how you feel as he pulls you into his arms for the hug he's longed for as he tells you he's planned a celebration just for you. He places an heirloom ring on your hand and pulls you toward the house to show you off. What do his actions show you about his love for you? How do you feel?

🐟 Why do you think Jesus gives us pictures of God's love for us instead of just telling us about him?

🐟 Describe a scene where this kind of father-love would heal a hurt in your life, then write a letter to God about it. He's running toward you to love you in this moment in your life.

Heart Cry

Dear God, help me see you as my perfect Father, apart from my misconceptions and wounds. I lay down my attempts to prove I'm good enough to earn your acceptance. Thank you for a love that surpasses any earthly father's love. Help me see myself as your child and live in that security.

Grieving and Growing

Will it ever be better, God?

I restore you.

My Child,
Even now I am creating a clean heart in you
and renewing a steadfast spirit in you.
I will not cast you away from my presence
or take my Holy Spirit from you.
I am restoring the joy of your salvation and
sustaining you with a willing spirit that is growing
in you day by day.

—YOUR LOVING FATHER
FROM PSALM 51:10–12

Longing for Home

My Father's house has many rooms; if that were not so, would I have told you that I am going there to prepare a place for you? And if I go and prepare a place for you, I will come back and take you to be with me that you also may be where I am. You know the way to the place where I am going.

JOHN 14:2–4

I'm dreaming my old, familiar daydream, God, of a happy family tucked away in a home with logs crackling in a fireplace, music filling the air, and cupboards filled to overflowing. I hear laughter and sense joy. In my dream I feel safe and protected—a reality that eluded me from the time I was a child.

I'm a grown woman, Lord, still longing for those feelings of safety and belonging. I drive through neighborhoods at dusk, looking through windows and imagining children safe and at play, protected and unthreatened—children wrapped in a womb of safety and love. The dream that began in childhood follows me like a shadow.

But the longing also brings back old, familiar feelings . . . the hopeless ache of abandonment. I feel the stinging emptiness as I long for the things I'll never have. My sadness in those moments overwhelms me, God.

When I was a little girl, you gave me four safe places to go to that I never wanted to leave: Auntie Margaret's, Auntie Susie's, my grandmother's, and my papa's house. No matter what dark secrets I was keeping or threats I was dodging, I always found safety, love, and protection in those special homes. They were gifts from you to my child's heart.

But like other children who felt as if they never belonged, I grew up and sometimes still long to feel safe and protected, God. My heart is still looking through windows for a place to call home. Is it possible for my heart to find a home, or is it too late?

Your longings are your heart's connection to your eternal home with me—longings for the security and belonging found in heaven. Your dream of safety and security is a taste of the peace you will one day experience fully in my presence. You long for nourishment of your body, soul, and spirit that can only be satisfied in me. You dream of nestling down in comfort and safety, knowing you are fully accepted and unconditionally loved.

Heaven is home, my child—where I will throw open my arms and embrace you, welcome you with a banquet, brag about you in front of your brothers and sisters, and walk you through the mansion I've prepared for you. Jesus himself will serve you out of his unfathomable grace and mercy, and you will be overwhelmed and fall at his feet. Love will flow in such abundance that angels' praise will fill eternity.

This is heaven, and I am your home.

I delight in giving you good things. I see your heart, and I know your dreams. Bring your dreams to me, and I will give you my desires to fill your heart.

It is never too late for dreams, my child. I hold your dreams in my hand, and I am the giver of all good gifts. Find your fulfillment in me, and trust me to tend your dreams out of the riches of my love for you.

Hope on the Edge

What about *home* does your heart long for that will be fulfilled in heaven?

God knows our deepest desires and wants the very best for us. What dreams has God fulfilled in your life or begun to fulfill? Why may the fulfillment of certain dreams be delayed right now?

Heart Cry

Dear God, I don't want to give up on my dreams. Give me dreams of your future for my life, and faith that you love me more than I can comprehend and that you want to bless me with good things. Make your home in me so that I can be a person who brings your hope and peace and love to others, no matter where I am or what material things I possess.

Tattered Hope

So we do not lose heart. Though our outer self is wasting
away, our inner self is being renewed day by day. For this light
momentary affliction is preparing for us an eternal weight of
glory beyond all comparison.
2 CORINTHIANS 4:16–17 ESV

My hope is tattered, God. Ripped like a rag and used to mop up the messes of my life.

How many times can a child be molested and still believe in anything good? Before I was five, I'd learned to send myself somewhere else in my mind to endure the abuse. When I was seven and stood on tiptoe to hang myself and failed, still I clung to you as a God who loved me. And when abuse came again and again at the hands of cousins and uncles who hid behind illusions of goodness and tortured children at will, I still clung to hope. When I thought I was finally safe for the hundredth time, and someone new tore another fragment of hope from my hands, I pressed the shredded threads of belief to my chest and still believed in you.

But lies stained the threads of faith, God. Torture makes children believe *they are* the evil, Lord. It makes them look for rocks and sticks to drive away the pain. Before I was eight, the rocks and sticks I chose were drugs, cutting, and burning. I didn't care that the weapons I chose to beat against my demons were hurting me, too.

My struggle was to get through the next day, the next hour, the next minute, even as I begged you to forgive the things I couldn't forgive in myself.

This world has torn me to shreds, Lord. Today I lay my tattered rags at your feet and ask you to give me new hope.

The hope you see as tattered is precious to me, my child, because it has cost you dearly. You offer me all you have. Your hope shines like diamonds and adorns the heavens.

The sin that touched you ripples into the lives of your family, community, and future generations. For this reason sin required an eternal solution that surpasses a single person and a single point in time. Jesus alone provided that eternal solution for you and all humanity.

Because of his completed work on your behalf, you are eternally, fully, irrevocably forgiven. My love, grace, and compassion flow out on you endlessly.

Before I shaped the stars, I loved you. Nothing you do can stir me to love you more or less.

You are not defined by the evil poured out on you. Jesus' blood covers and shields you. His righteousness and holiness shine from you with such brilliance that the angels are humbled in your presence.

I give you wholeness and healing for your tatters, my child. The tatters of your hope have been sown into the tapestry of Jesus' righteousness and sufficiency. Cling to my promise that the hope, healing, and future I have secured for you exceed and surpass what you see and understand.

Hope on the Edge

If you've struggled with self-abuse, help is available. The first step is often talking about your pain. Cutting, burning, and other forms of self-harm are often symptoms of PTSD and can be effectively addressed through trauma treatment. Help is available through the resources found in appendix 3 or at http://www.self-injury.org/.

In what ways has your hope been tattered? What hope is God whispering to you in this moment?

Heart Cry

Dear Father, I claim wholeness I cannot see and love I often cannot feel. I claim purpose in pain and offer forgiveness to those who don't deserve it. I will fight my negative self-talk and see myself the way you see me—beautiful and holy. Give me wisdom to see the negative patterns I've created and to move forward into wise thinking and behaviors.

The Asterisk

You will surely forget your trouble,
recalling it only as waters gone by.
Life will be brighter than noonday,
and darkness will become like morning.
You will be secure, because there is hope;
you will look about you and take your rest in safety.

JOB 11:16–18

I know you don't lie, God. I've pretty much staked my life on the fact that the Bible is true and I can count on it. But here's my biggest problem with believing you. I know you say there's healing and hope for messed-up people. That's why Jesus died on the cross, right? For everyone, right?

And I know he died for me. But something inside my head tells me I'm the asterisk in the Bible—the one person who's the exception. The one who really can't be healed. The one who's blown it so bad that I'll never be able to get it right.

From the outside, I can look like I'm doing great. A successful career. Great family and friends. A Christian with a relationship with you.

But on the inside I'm broken, unraveling, tattered, and faded. I don't want anyone to get close enough to see the ugliness. I live with the terror that I'm unfixable, God.

I want to trust you because I *know* you're the God who heals.

You healed in the past, and you heal today. But my feelings tell me I'm irreparably broken and not worth trying to save. It's terrifying to think I'm the one person truly beyond your reach.

I don't want to be right, and I don't want to live with this terror. I want to feel loved. I want to feel treasured. And I want to believe that you have hope for even me.

My Dear Child,

Feelings are important, but they are an ever-changing measure of reality. Feelings are based on your limited perception of your world. Like a child looking out a window, you can only see the view from one side of the glass. But I see your world from above—where the horizon meets the sky and where the east meets the west.

Whether or not you feel loved, you *are* loved. The fact that you are loved by me cannot change because I never change. Your feelings are not part of the equation of my perfect love. Behaving badly will not make me love you less, and performing all the good works in the world could never make me love you more.

Yes, you've blown it so badly that you may never "get it right." Every man, woman, and child ever conceived is equally unrighteous. No one has ever or could ever live life without falling short of my perfect standard—except Jesus. But because I exchanged his complete righteousness for your total unworthiness, you stand before me totally spotless and without blame.

When I look at you, I see sinless perfection. Like a parent with a newborn child, I love you so much that I could look at you and brag about you forever, and I plan to do just that. My father-heart bursts with pride over you!

You are treasured. You are adored. You are my own, my beloved. Whether or not you ever feel those things, they are eternally true.

Hope on the Edge

Have you ever felt like the asterisk in the Bible—the exception to God's love and grace? How does this fly in the face of Scripture?

Describe what it feels like to know that you cannot disappoint God and that he takes delight in you.

Heart Cry

Abba Father, today I choose to believe you are an adoring father bragging about me, his newborn child. I choose truth over feelings. And I choose to walk in my identity as chosen, redeemed, claimed, and perfected through the blood of Jesus. Let that knowledge give me a new joy in my life.

Betrayal

Rejoice not over me, O my enemy;
when I fall, I shall rise;
when I sit in darkness,
the LORD will be a light to me.
MICAH 7:8 ESV

How is it, God, that some mothers and fathers can abandon their children?

What monster rages in the hearts of people that men and women can sacrifice their children on the altar of evil?

Who can we trust, God, when the people who are supposed to love and protect us betray us?

Betrayal suffocates the soul. Trust is the soil that feeds faith. It nourishes our sense of safety and security. Trust tells the spirit that it's okay to relax, breathe deeply, and rest. But betrayal strips all that is nourishing from relationships and leaves nothing but parched, dry dust.

And here, in this desert of betrayal, my dry bones withered with a thirst for love to be poured into my spirit, God.

I'm coming to you and praying that the love you promise, God, is not a mirage.

Dear Child,

People often believe that mothers and fathers who abandon or harm their children are special kinds of sinners. But sin runs so deeply in the hearts of mankind that everyone is capable of the most desperate and despicable sin. People do not see these things in themselves because they are blind to their capacity for evil and have not all been subject to the same combinations of genetics, circumstances, generational influences, choices, and consequences of others' sin.

I turned my face away from my Son as he died an agonizing death and took on the sins of all humanity. Jesus took the greatest evil, perversion, and degradation upon himself and gave his life for the world so that every man, woman, and child who comes to me in simple faith can be forgiven and live free. So that you can know that freedom.

Humanity betrayed Jesus and turned away. Their rejection sent him to the cross. And day after day those I created to love me still turn and walk away.

I am here right now. I am not a mirage or a myth. I am pouring out my love for you in a never-ending river.

And I long for you to love me in return, my precious one.

Hope on the Edge

Have you struggled with feelings of abandonment? What lies have you grappled with as a result? Your soul longs to know that someone will never leave you—someone who will love you unconditionally and relentlessly. Read the following verses: Psalm 37:28; Joshua 1:5; Isaiah 49:15–16; Leviticus 26:11–12. What do these verses say about God's never-failing love and commitment to you?

God "engraved you on the palms of [his] hands"; he indelibly marked into his very person. Meditate on this image that God chose to communicate his commitment to you.

Heart Cry

Dear God, it hurts so much to know that people who are supposed to love me hurt me. You know what betrayal feels like because you chose it when you didn't have to. Thank you for coming to my rescue, and help me see that rescue isn't always about taking me out of my circumstances but learning to trust you in those circumstances.

Releasing the Death Grip

If anyone says, "I love God," and hates his brother, he is a liar;
for he who does not love his brother whom he has seen cannot
love God whom he has not seen.

1 JOHN 4:20 ESV

I never knew how much I could hate until someone molested my child, God.

Not once. Not twice. Not three times. How does a mother even ask her child how many times someone has abused her?

And it wasn't a stranger, it was a friend. Someone I trusted like family. When I first heard he might have victimized my child, I felt guilty even thinking it could be true.

But it was, and when I realized what he'd done, I wanted to throw up. Then my feelings turned to rage, and I wanted to kill him. Not just for a week or a month, but for years. I attended church and politely nodded at the pastor's sermons.

My soul still clings to my rage in a death grip, God, and I don't want to let go, even though I know I should. I've heard sermons on forgiveness, but I want justice. I wonder how someone who's done such things could deserve forgiveness or grace. Isn't forgiveness that's free to everyone for everything a cheap excuse for forgiveness? Shouldn't it cost us something?

Something inside me cries out for blood. But even that won't wash away my child's scars and pain.

What happened to your child is a horrific sin that tears my heart. The Enemy of her soul planned to destroy her through this assault, but I can assure you I have a greater purpose, and she is not a powerless victim. Even evil can be used to strengthen her, increase her faith, and draw others to me if she trusts me to accomplish these things in her.

People wrongly deceive themselves into thinking they are good because they disguise their capacity for sin. Becoming the object of others' sin has a way of drawing out mankind's bent and twisted nature. Yes, something deep within you cries out for blood. That same cry echoes within the hearts of all men and women, and only the covering of Jesus' sinless blood can satisfy it.

No one deserves forgiveness. All humanity stands shoulder-to-shoulder before me, no more or less deserving of my grace. And so, my child, when you say you love me, I see the evidence reflected in the way you forgive others.

Learn my grace, and allow it to move you to love. Love will move you to forgiveness. Forgiveness does not negate accountability and consequences. Seek those things as you rest in my promise of final justice.

Hope on the Edge

When those we love are hurt, something inside us cries out for pay-back. We believe that justice will somehow set things right again. When have you asked God for justice against someone who has hurt you or a loved one? Did justice come in a way that drew you or others closer to God?

God tells us that he forgives us with the same measure we forgive those who have sinned against us (Matthew 6:14–15). How does this truth influence the way you interact with those who've wronged you?

Heart Cry

Dear God, help me see the sin in my own heart and the overwhelming love and forgiveness you've given me. May the enormity of your gift cause me to overflow with forgiveness for even my enemies. Help me release the bitterness and anger. I lay down my self-righteousness and release to you the people who've wronged me. Replace my bitterness with a gratitude that changes the way I look at the world and see the people around me.

Speaking Truth to Broken Places

Read Psalm 51:1–17

When we live with the aftermath of trauma, we can sometimes lash out and hurt people. We may be stuck in cycles of depression, addiction, victimization, rage, or compulsive behaviors that harm the people we love—intentionally or unintentionally.

True Guilt

Survivors of trauma struggle with true guilt and false guilt. To understand the difference, we must recognize that guilt is both a feeling and an objective reality. Healthy, true guilt comes from a sense of right and wrong that is rooted in the Bible. Healthy guilt tells us when we've done something morally, ethically, or legally wrong. And it's intended to move us in a direction that causes us to resolve it, so we tend to feel awful or experience conflicted emotions until we resolve our guilt. This is one function of the conscience, in cooperation with the Holy Spirit, God places within us.

However, the "feeling" of guilt is an unreliable standard. For instance, I might steal a cookie and not feel guilt, but from a biblical standpoint, I'm guilty of the act.

False Guilt

We can also feel guilty because other people impose their expectations on us or we're trying to prove something. False guilt is unrelated to a standard of right and wrong, or it can mean taking on responsibility that doesn't belong to us. It's easy for false guilt to become a burden for children who grow up in homes where addiction is part of the culture. Children often take on parental roles and feel guilty for not performing tasks that belong to their parents. False guilt can also come because we have an improper sense of identity, haven't established appropriate boundaries, don't have a clear understanding of right and wrong, or misunderstand our roles.

Written on Our Hearts

🐾 In what ways have you struggled with false guilt as a result of trauma or abuse? What effect has this had on you? On others?

🐾 In what ways have you struggled with true guilt because of abuse? Read Psalm 51:1–17.

🐾 Which phrases record what the psalmist will do or the part he contributes as he comes to God, asking for forgiveness (vv. 13, 15, 17)?

🐾 Which phrases record what the psalmist asks of God (vv. 1–2, 7–12, 14–15)?

🐾 What qualities of God does the psalmist recognize (vv. 1, 4, 6, 10, 12, 14)?

- What qualities of spirit does the psalmist approach God with (vv. 1–17)?

- Imagine yourself sitting as a child on God's lap as he speaks truth to your broken places. What is he saying to you—as a child? As a teenager? At the various points of pain in your life as an adult? What do you want to say back to him?

Heart Cry

Lord, teach me wisdom that lays down false guilt and uses true guilt to change my life and show me how to love people better as I become more like Jesus.

I bless you with the power to forgive.

Dear Child,
If you forgive those who sin against you,
I will forgive you.
But if you refuse to forgive others,
even your worst enemies,
I will not forgive your sins.

—YOUR GRACIOUS FATHER
FROM MATTHEW 6:14–15

Daddy's Girl

See what kind of love the Father has given to us, that we should
be called children of God; and so we are.
1 JOHN 3:1 ESV

Dear God,

My earthly father wasn't perfect. Nobody is, I guess. But deep inside, I wanted him to see me, to listen, to hear my heart.

I think he tried. He just didn't know how.

Dad *did* see my grades. He saw my weight. He saw when I colored outside the lines. He saw my failures. He saw himself in everything I did.

But he never saw *me*—the inside of me—my fears and insecurities and dreams. The things that made me cry in the night and the things deep in a daughter's heart she wants to tell her father. I tried to tell him those things, but he didn't know how to listen, so I stopped trying.

I learned how to gain his approval doing "good Christian things," and all the while I prayed that someday he'd finally see the little girl who just wanted to sit on his lap and whisper her dreams in his ear.

Those days have passed, God. I know now I can't do enough, that I can't be enough, that I can't fill that hole. The little girl inside me is tired of tugging on his shirtsleeve and praying to be seen. The adult me still sits in a corner and cries.

Dearest Daughter,

Your father was a broken child. He loved you very much, but he struggled to see beyond his hurts. If you listen, you can learn the love language he tried so hard to speak to you. My child, he wanted you to love him, but his needs drove him to grasp, instead of show grace.

The deepest desire of every human being is to be seen and known. Your desire to be seen by your father is rooted to a deeper desire to be seen and known by me, your heavenly Father.

Part of you is still a child with an abandoned heart. Part of you is still a teenager, furious that her father does not listen. Part of you is still a resigned thirty-four-year-old who has given up the dream of ever knowing her daddy.

I speak healing to every wounded part of you. I hear your every heart cry. My heart breaks with you in your pain. Not a single thought of your heart escapes my notice. I will never reject or forsake you.

I will turn your weeping into dancing and renew your strength as you lean on me—your unfailing Father who sees and adores you.

Hope on the Edge

We are the sum total of every day we've ever lived and every age we've ever been. Even though we may be middle-aged, we're still a wounded child, a frustrated teenager, and all the experiences we've ever lived. Jesus speaks healing to every broken place and counters the lies that flow from those wounds. Ask him to speak to those parts of your wounded spirit and listen as he offers you healing. Use appendix 6 to assist you.

Journal your responses.

Heart Cry

Dear God, help me forgive the people who disappointed me and hurt me. Help me grant them the same grace you have granted me. Help me see the broken people around me as you see them and call them to become that person instead of looking to them to fulfill my needs.

The Longest Ride

The Spirit of God has made me,
and the breath of the Almighty gives me life.
JOB 33:4 ESV

I've tried to fill this hole in my soul for too many years, Lord. You know I've tried to forget, but some things just can't be forgotten . . . shouldn't be forgotten, no matter how much they hurt.

Can you forgive me for killing my unborn baby, Lord? For not changing my mind on the longest ride of my life . . . for not refusing to open the door . . . for not running from the waiting room?

Does it matter that I felt trapped? Threatened? Scared? That it seemed like there was no way out and no one cared? And that when it was over, I wanted to curl into a ball and die myself?

I'm tortured by questions . . . not knowing if my baby was a girl or a boy. Not knowing if she'd look like that little girl smiling at me across her mother's shoulder or that little boy with a streak of dirt across his cheek waving at me from a grocery cart. And worst of all, not knowing if my child will ever forgive me.

I've carried this hidden secret, and it's eating away at me. Part of me died that day. Can you forgive me, Lord, and breathe life back into this empty part of my soul?

Of course you can be forgiven, my child. But the greater question is whether you *are* forgiven *right now*. Are you truly my child? Have you asked forgiveness of your sins and come into a relationship with me? Yes, your abortion was a sin, but abortion is not a special category of offense that is less forgivable to me. When you became my child, you were declared righteous in my sight, regardless of your sins. Every day my Holy Spirit works in you, making you more and more like Jesus.

Along with forgiveness, I grant cleansing, which not only changes your relationship with me, but also changes the reality of who you are. You have a clean heart, my child, as spotless as the heart of Jesus.

Having an abortion does not mean you are evil. The choices of your past do not define who you are. This is the hope and freedom that comes with salvation—I give you new life and a new identity. You cannot earn forgiveness—it is my free gift to you.

You possess the heart of a loving mother, and your child knows the wonder of being in the presence of my perfect love.

My heart is stirred by your heartache for the loss of your child and your suffering. Your decision cost you dearly. I, too, loved and lost a child to death because of the pain inflicted by the world. I know the tearing agony of separation. But Jesus' death and resurrection broke the curse of death for all mankind.

Breathe freely, child, and feel the life of my Spirit flow through you and wash away your shame. You are forgiven, accepted, and loved beyond measure.

Hope on the Edge

Do you carry shame and guilt over the burden of a hidden sin? You've not only been forgiven, you've been cleansed from your sin. First John 1:9 says that if we confess our sin, God is faithful to cleanse us from *all* unrighteousness. Envision yourself standing pure and spotless before God as he smiles at you in approval. What does this feel like?

How do your life and thinking change when you walk in the freedom of forgiveness?

Heart Cry

Dear God, thank you for the gift of forgiveness that frees me from shame. Thank you for your unconditional love and compassion. Help me believe and live out the truth that you blot out our sins and that I live free from guilt.

When the Ring Comes Off

Great is his love toward us,
and the faithfulness of the LORD endures forever.
PSALM 117:2

Dear God,

I know the verses and the promises. Today is the day you made, and I'm supposed to rejoice. But joy doesn't seem possible today.

You know what day it is, Lord. One year ago today the heavily-invested-in life that I'd spent years and tears building exploded into a million pieces.

One year ago.

I remember when twelve months seemed like such a l-o-n-g time, but I can tell you now that time can move so fast that it can make the world look unreal . . . like a figment of the imagination.

Some days I feel like my marriage was a figment of my imagination, God. It's been a year since everything I thought I knew was blown to bits by just a few words: "I love someone else."

I never expected the word *love* to shatter my soul with the force of a grenade.

I'm frustrated with myself for the pain I still feel a year later.

How could twelve years spent side-by-side sharing my life with someone be tossed out as if it were nothing? Who does that? I tried to do all the right things. I know I wasn't perfect, but I loved my husband and tried to give him a beautiful home and make sure he wanted for nothing. I prayed for us every day and believed you'd given us an ever-after kind of love.

But none of it mattered, and I don't know how to be okay with that. The one person in this world I gave myself to completely and trusted more than anyone else betrayed and humiliated me without apology, and a year later I'm still unable to move past the pain. I don't know how not to feel abandoned, and I don't even want to know how to be alone.

I'm angry. I don't understand what happened. Please help me heal, God, and move past this place.

Dearest Daughter,

Divorce is a tearing apart of souls and bodies joined as one, and it comes with enormous cost and horrific pain. I detest divorce because it causes wrenching pain for my children and mars their spirits at the core. The unity of marriage reflects my bond with my beloved bride, the church. The awareness that you were created for eternal oneness is stamped upon your very being.

You were betrayed, my child, and anger has its time and place. I am angry along with you for lies, dishonor, neglect, and abandonment. But allow anger to move you toward healing and toward me. Moving forward often means leaving things behind and setting your eyes on things beyond. Lift your eyes, my child, and look ahead. I call you to a hope and a future.

Look deep within as well, daughter. Explore your heart and your motives. Do not be afraid of what you might find, for I will meet you there. I am well pleased with you. You delight my heart. Use this time to journey to a deeper place of forgiveness and self-knowledge, and I will show you truth that will move you past this place and set you free through the power of my Spirit in you.

I love you, precious one. You are not alone.

Hope on the Edge

Satan wants you to feel as though you failed and are a failure. In what ways have you struggled with these feelings? God says you are accepted and loved unconditionally. What words are reflected by unconditional love and acceptance? Write them down as God's message of love to you.

Read Psalm 117:2. Imagine God speaking these words to you. What do they mean to you?

Heart Cry

Dear God, help me remember that rejection and abandonment do not define me. They are the product of sin. My value is defined by who you say I am. I am adored, embraced, secure, and approved in your love. No matter what I may do or not do, you will never divorce me or leave me, God, because your love never fails. Heal my heart, and give me courage to look inside and use this pain to move me forward as I grow in Jesus.

The Brown Robe

The LORD himself goes before you and will be with you;
he will never leave you nor forsake you. Do not be afraid;
do not be discouraged.

As a mother-in-waiting, I welcomed my first labor pains. I was exhilarated. Terrified. And shocked that having a baby could hurt so much.

My labor stretched into hours, then days. You heard my prayers, God. When the doctor decided to take my baby by C-section, I breathed a sigh of relief.

But the anesthesia crept into my lungs. I was sure I was going to die, Lord. As the doctor shoved a tube down my throat, my last thought was that I'd never live to hold my baby.

My husband and I brought a daughter home a week later, but I also came home with depression. I struggled to get out of bed and seldom changed out of my brown robe. I stared into space, didn't answer the phone, and couldn't focus.

I felt so guilty, God. New mothers are supposed to be happy, but I felt numb. Good Christian women were supposed to be joy-filled, right? How could I admit I was struggling with despair?

Years later, someone would explain that my brain had been overwhelmed by trauma during my child's birth. It took my body more than a year to recover, but for decades I suffered with guilt about my "failure" as a new mother.

Sometimes I still fear I failed my child, my husband, and you, Lord. I'd like to believe that even though you see my failures, I can one day finally walk away from my guilt. And that I can learn to be honest with those who've shamed me for admitting my depression, as though it's a spiritual failure.

Give me wisdom to know how to grant forgiveness and grace to others who don't understand depression. Give me wisdom to know how to speak the truth in love. Help me remember that depression is not something to be forgiven in myself but something even Jesus shared with me.

Dear One,

As a man, Jesus experienced the agony of separation from loved ones, of abandonment, of physical suffering. He willingly came to earth to experience all that humanity experienced—even depression.

I understand the complex way your body responds to crisis. I created amazing mechanisms within your anatomy for self-healing and protection. You were depleted by your experience and did not understand what happened to you. You felt shame over your body's biological responses to your birth experience, and you felt isolated and alone.

I am with you and for you in every experience. Nothing is too small to bring to me. Nothing is too shameful. Nothing will cause me to turn away from you. Nothing can make me love you more or less. As you struggled through your long hours of depression, I sat at your side and heard your every whisper of self-doubt and self-accusation.

My child, you are beloved and accepted. Walk away from your guilt by walking in your true identity: You are loved in me. Forgiveness is granted for sin, my child. Illness is to be met with compassion.

Drink deeply from the blessings of the Spirit to refresh your soul. Grow in wisdom as you sit with me and learn to trust my love for you.

Hope on the Edge

Most women will struggle with depression at some point in their lives. If this has been part of your journey or the journey of someone dear to you, what did you do to cope? How did you handle the emotions and the physical symptoms?

Use the words of Deuteronomy 31:8 to write a letter from God's heart to yours.

Heart Cry

Father, you have not forgotten me, no matter how I feel. I choose to come to you and move toward you. Help me trust more in your character and less in what I see and understand. You are my refuge in the good times and the bad, and I rejoice in you.

The Sound of the Closing Door

For when we came into Macedonia, we had no rest, but we were
harassed at every turn—conflicts on the outside, fears within.
But God, who comforts the downcast, comforted us by the
coming of Titus, and not only by his coming but also by the
comfort you had given him.

2 CORINTHIANS 7:5–7

Today I watched as a woman stood at a wrought-iron gate, wiggling the lock handle until it slid into place. The squeaking and clanging of the door and the scrape of metal against metal startled me, and I froze. Instantly, I was six years old and standing in the middle of one of the worst memories of my life—a moment that changed my life forever.

God, remembering that scene today overwhelmed me and made me want to disappear. Like other triggers from my past, the sight and sound shook me and made me sick as memories pounded through my head. Once again, I was held hostage as flashbacks took me back to that place I've tried so hard to forget.

The clang of the gate separated me from the most important people in my life. I never knew if they'd come for me again. I was abandoned and alone. The sadness of that moment is so profound my body aches and my head goes numb with pain. The fear of being forgotten . . . of being unwanted . . . pushes me into a scary, silent place deep within me.

I don't want to lose myself in this deep sadness every time I'm ambushed by that hated noise.

I don't want to feel six years old again and stand terrified in that place where people leave me behind and moms and dads walk away into the unknown. Once was enough.

God, free me from the torment of triggers that keep me chained to the past—that hurt my heart and shatter my soul over and over again. Show me if my heart holds traces of unforgiveness, and then please help me forgive. I'm willing, Lord. Please heal me.

My Child,

I never grow weary or annoyed when you come to me with your heartache. I never tire of listening to the things you whisper or scream or plead or have no words for. This ache you feel . . . this feeling of abandonment . . . is rooted to the core of your being. It is rooted to your desire to be known and loved. It is rooted to me.

Thank you for coming to me with this prayer. It is precious to me.

You have asked for healing, but your understanding of healing is limited, my child. I have provided for your healing in ways that surpass the confines of your understanding. And because of this, the healing I provide does not always come in a manner you understand or on the timeline you desire.

The healing you ask for is the removal of something painful. But often the journey to healing unlocks gifts far greater than the healing itself. Through the power of my Spirit, I empower you for a day-by-day walk that draws you closer to me and teaches you to better love yourself and others. In those moments when you are triggered, a wounded part of you cries out to be heard. Quiet your heart and listen, my child, to the broken part of you. Listen for my voice of love, grace, and truth in that broken place. This is the healing I desire for you—to see yourself as loved, seen, known, and embraced by me in your deepest pain.

Trust me. Your healing has already been enacted both on earth and in heaven. Through the blood of Jesus, I have healed you. I am healing you. And I will continue to heal you.

You have asked me to help you forgive. Your open heart is the first step. Let your heart be moved by love and gratitude for the gift of my forgiveness. Forgiveness follows a heart that is moved by love. As soon as you obey, your heart is moved to greater faith.

Although you may feel chained to the past, you are held in my hands, and you are growing into the beautiful daughter I have called you to be.

You are safe. Eternally secure. Written upon my hands and my heart. Eternally loved.

Hope on the Edge
How have triggers influenced your life? In what ways have your triggers made you feel separated from others and from God?

Where have you sought the most effective healing for your triggers? If you have not pursued trauma therapy, begin by reading appendix 1 and then investigate and pray about the approach that might work best for you.

Heart Cry
Dear God, I feel trapped by triggers that seem to control my life. Help me remember that you are in control, no matter what I feel. Your love has stamped me with your irrevocable identity. I am free to

seek treatment for my trauma from the best professionals available, as you speak love, acceptance, peace, security, and identity to my soul for the healing of my heart.

Forgiving Ourselves
Read Psalm 103:8–12

Forgiving ourselves can often be the toughest thing we ever do. Satan loves to make us believe we're beyond hope and chained to our past. And it's easy to buy the lie.

The simple truth is that every time the voice in our head tells us we don't deserve God's grace, it's right. That's why it's called *grace*. *Grace* is "unmerited favor from God" or "a gift we don't deserve."

Unmerited favor. Something we can never earn. A gift beyond our ability to ever gain for ourselves.

Strangely Silent?
You can search the Bible and never find verses about how to forgive yourself. Doesn't sound like much help, right? The truth is that when we focus on trying to forgive ourselves, we take our eyes off God, where the attention belongs. Of course we sin. We're messed up, and deep inside we know it, but we just can't seem to get our eyes off our failures.

But God says, "Look at me. Be blown away by how much I love you. Let my love for you overwhelm you."

Written on Our Hearts
God's character is love. Read Psalm 103:1–8.

🐟 What characteristics describe God's love for us?

🐟 Read 1 John 1:9. When God says he forgives us from "all" of our sins and "all" unrighteousness, do voices in your head immediately say you're an exception? For what sins or actions?

🐟 In what ways do you think Satan wins and God loses when you limit God's grace?

When we say we don't feel forgiven, we're saying that Jesus' death on the cross wasn't enough to pay for our sins. We have to do something more, and we can't trust God when he says his grace is sufficient for everyone.

🐟 In what ways would living and breathing a grace-filled life free you to live differently? In what ways would embracing this truth free you from your past and move you toward God's vision for your future?

First John 1:9 promises God has "purified" us. This purification rests in the finished work of Jesus, not in anything we can ever accomplish. If you've accepted Jesus as your Savior, you've been washed and cleansed.

🐟 Write a letter of forgiveness to yourself. Express your feelings freely, including your remorse or anger for the things you have done. Ask God if there are steps that are necessary for you to complete to bring reconciliation or restoration between yourself and others. Then create a ceremony of closure—perhaps burning the letter—and replacing it with a love letter from God.

Heart Cry

Dear Father, I'm having trouble forgiving myself, and I ask you to cleanse me and forgive me for unconfessed sin. Because I'm your precious child and Jesus paid the price for my sin, I can face you openly and freely without fear. Thank you for loving me unconditionally. I refuse to walk under self-inflicted shame and condemnation and cheapen your love for me. Today I claim the grace you've given me by walking in freedom.

I secure you in my love.

Dear One,
You called out to me, and I heard you.
I saved you
when the cords of death entangled you
and the torrents of destruction overwhelmed you.
The cords of the grave coiled around you
and the snares of death confronted you,
but I came to your rescue.

—YOUR LOVING FATHER
FROM PSALM 18:3–5

Just One More Time

Anyone who does not provide for their relatives,
and especially for their own household, has denied the faith
and is worse than an unbeliever.

1 TIMOTHY 5:8

For more than three years, I was afraid to speak the word out loud. *Alzheimer's.*

But the hard truth was that my mother was going to die a slow, agonizing death.

You know how hard my father, my brother, our spouses and children all tried to push back the inevitable march of death, Lord.

No son or daughter wants to think about the things they may be called upon to do for their aging parents in the name of love. To my mother's diseased mind, my caregiving must have looked like torture at times. It often felt that way to me as I blocked her blows and calmed her cries.

I didn't know how to watch my mom suffer, God. I didn't know how to help her die. I didn't know how to listen to her beg for release from torment. And I didn't know how to say good-bye after watching her wither away over nearly a dozen years.

I did all I knew to do, God, and prayed every day that somewhere, in spite of the chaos in her head, Mom knew that the family who loved her never left her side.

Today her pink robe hanging in the spare bedroom closet ambushed me, and I couldn't stop crying. Even though I know Mom's with you, I still ache to tell her I love her one more time.

I saw everything you did in the name of love, my child. Every act of seeming insignificance was weighted with eternal glory. You tended to your mother's deepest needs, even when she was not aware of them. You grieved for her. And you sacrificed your own life out of sheer love like Jesus.

You delight my heart, and all heaven hears me brag about you. Here with me, your mother knows your love more fully and completely than she ever knew it on earth.

You grieve deeply because you loved deeply. I did not intend for earthly relationships to be severed. Death is a temporary tearing apart that has fallen upon humanity as one consequence of sin. Be blessed in anticipating a sweet reunion with your mother here with me and Jesus, whose life-gift pours strength into you even now.

You did not fight a powerless battle against your mother's illness. You showed the world and your mother the face of love and faithfulness—my face. You won the greatest battle—sowing life and purpose into the lives of those around you.

Hope on the Edge

We can battle against death alongside those we love and still lose. Have you gotten angry with God because you lost loved ones? Consider writing him a letter that tells him how you feel. Then write out a letter in return that states what your loved one would tell you today.

Read Isaiah 53:3–5. What do these verses say about the lengths God went to for you because he loves you?

Heart Cry

Dear Father, sometimes my grief seems too much to bear. Help me treasure the past without getting stuck there. And help me make my way through the grief while giving myself permission to acknowledge my pain and the loss. Forgive me for the mistake of ever blaming you for suffering instead of seeing you as my Savior in the suffering.

Safe

Let the beloved of the LORD rest secure in him,
for he shields him all day long,
and the one the LORD loves rests between his shoulders.
DEUTERONOMY 33:12

God, I don't feel safe, and it terrifies me. So I protect myself by creating "rules."

I'm not allowed to be afraid.

I'm not allowed to feel abandoned or forgotten.

And if I fail and break my own rules, I punish myself.

I've been trying for years to convince myself it doesn't matter what people think and that I don't care. But the thing is, I do care and I'm afraid—afraid of disappointing everyone and losing them.

God, when I was a little girl and afraid, I closed my eyes and squeezed them tight until I could see a picture in my head. In this picture, I crawled onto your lap and rested my head on your shoulder and nuzzled my face into your neck. I sat there while you stroked my head and whispered softly that I was loved and I was yours. I've done that many times over the years, and it's the only thing that makes me feel safe enough to get through my worst days and nights.

Even though that picture only exists inside my head, I've always felt safest imagining myself with you. No matter how old I get, I never lose the desire to crawl onto your lap, God, and have you whisper to me that you're keeping me safe.

When I created you, child, I created you so we could communicate without speaking a word. You are tied to me through the power of your thoughts, unspoken words, and imagination. When you see me holding you and speaking words of love and assurance, I *am* with you. Your ability to envision my presence as a comforter and healer is one of my gifts to you.

I see the five-year-old child inside you who is frightened and feels abandoned. I see every event that scarred you and left you broken and battling the lies that call out to your spirit. But my Spirit is with you to comfort you with truth to counter the lies.

I will never turn you away. You will never grow too old to come to me with your fears and approach me as a child approaches a father. Even the most well-intentioned earthly father will fail his child, but I will never fail you. I will never turn my back on you. My love for you is limitless and cannot be measured or compared to anything you have seen or experienced.

So come to me, child. Crawl into the safety of my arms. Whisper to me and know that I hang on your every word.

And when you are weary with exhaustion and feel you cannot take another breath, lean back and know that I am holding you securely in my arms.

Hope on the Edge
When have you created your own "rules" to protect yourself? What have they looked like? Why have they failed you in the end?

God shields us from the full force of Satan's deadly intentions against us. When have you been able to gain a glimpse of this protection? If you've never thanked God, do it now.

Heart Cry
Help me trust you to keep me safe, God, even when I don't feel safe. Give me faith to come to you when circumstances tell me you're not there and to trust the things I can do myself. Help me remember that you're always listening, you always care, and you're always acting for my good. Thank you for never tiring of carrying me.

The Food Feud

*We demolish arguments and every pretension that sets itself up
against the knowledge of God, and we take captive every thought
to make it obedient to Christ.*

2 CORINTHIANS 10:5

I'm so ashamed. Once again, the bear claw won.

My dismal record of 0–23 against this clawed pastry has me on the floor, shaking my head in disgust. I know I'm not the only one who struggles with addiction, God. I know other Christians battle and lose to other things—alcohol, sex, drugs, shopping, pornography . . . nothing can fill us or heal our soul-sickness.

So here I am with almond paste on my face and nowhere to turn as once again the truth of my inability to win this battle hits me. Ouch.

God, my seemingly eternal battle with food is killing me. Literally. This abusive relationship is making me sick and destroying my body—your temple. It's robbing me of energy and health and life. But I just can't seem to do the things I know I need to do.

And here's where I go off the rails. Just as I commit to finally getting my eating under control, I find myself celebrating because I got a Burger King coupon in the mail!

If this compulsion wasn't killing me, my life would be a great comedy show. But the truth is, I'm dying.

I know I need to learn how to fight this addiction a new way, Lord. I just don't know how.

You were born hungry, daughter. Everyone is born with a deep craving, and they spend their lives pursuing *more*.

More power.

More sex.

More money.

More peace.

But what they're really searching for is the Ultimate—Me.

Burritos, Whoppers, chocolate, exercise, shopping, gambling, sex, porn, and alcohol will always leave you wanting more. I created you with a longing for me that nothing on earth can fill. But the hurts of this world create cravings that consume your soul. Hunger is a mirror that shows you your need for me. Welcome it.

My Holy Spirit empowers you for all good things. Jesus is the Bread of Life. He infuses you with inner strength through the power of the Spirit. Addiction is the place where you are forced to throw up your hands and give everything to me or live out of your own sufficiency.

I am not asking you to give up bear claws. I am asking you to give *all of yourself* to me. To offer yourself as a living sacrifice, simply because you love me, out of pure love.

That is *my* desire.

Hope on the Edge

What addictions have held you captive? How have they influenced your life?

What do you need to release so that you can give all of yourself to God? What are first steps on this journey?

Heart Cry

God, help me love you so much that I'm willing to give you the things I tell myself are satisfying the drive for *more* inside of me. May I give you the first and best of all I have because my love for you won't allow me to do anything less.

Fighting the Feelings

Before a word is on my tongue
you, LORD, know it completely.
You hem me in behind and before,
and you lay your hand upon me.

PSALM 139:4–5

I've always felt like the abuse was my fault, God. Year after year, the what-ifs pound through my head.

What if I hadn't . . .
What if I had . . .
If only I'd . . .

I didn't deserve what was done to me, but the child inside me tells me if I'd just been better . . . just done things differently, life wouldn't have come crashing down.

Shame and guilt rule my life, Lord. Anxiety. Self-hatred. Rage. Are Christian women allowed to admit we sometimes don't feel virtuous? That anger and bitterness sometimes sweep us away, even though we love you and long to please you?

No one understands how I feel, Lord. How many times have I been told to pray harder, have more faith, trust you more? You know how hard I've tried . . . how hard I'm trying. But the self-condemning voices are still there, and I'm still struggling. So I withdraw in silence and shame, but even in my shame, I'm drawn to you.

Here I am, Lord, asking *What if* one more time. *What if* you really do love me? And *what if* you can wash away these feelings?

My Child,

Emotions help you create meaning from the world. They help you understand who you are and your relationship to people and to me. But by themselves, emotions are not trustworthy. They must be filtered through truth that is rooted in me and my Word.

Jesus loved people and felt compassion. When Lazarus died, Jesus grieved, even though he had the power to raise him. Jesus agonized over his own death in the garden of Gethsemane, knowing the immeasurable price he would pay. Yet his emotions were never overruled by selfish desires, sinful motives, or his personal agenda.

The road you find yourself on has not diverted you from my plans. You are not lost or out of my care. While it may look to you as though evil has won, your destiny rests securely in my hands.

Like a child in the back seat of a vehicle on a long trip, you can only see what is inside the car and outside your window. But I see your vehicle, the road you are traveling and all the roads that connect to it, earth's terrain and the weather patterns swirling above you, the solar system, the galaxies, the universe and beyond, and the parameters of eternity that embrace you. I hold you in the palm of my hand.

You are safe. You are loved. You are never out of my care. Those words are the greatest truth you can ever believe—even when you do not feel them.

Hope on the Edge
How has Satan bound you to the past with what-if thinking?

Using the affirmations found in appendix 6, write out a new list of what-ifs for your life. For instance, what if I saw myself as forgiven and free? How would the way I lived today change? Then pray and ask the Spirit of God to help you walk in the truth of that reality.

Heart Cry
Dear God, when negative feelings overwhelm me, help me believe what is true, noble, right, pure, lovely, of good report, admirable, excellent, and praiseworthy—even when those things are hard to believe. Help me remind myself I am safe and loved by you.

No Place to Run

"Look! God's dwelling place is now among the people, and he will dwell with them. They will be his people, and God himself will be with them and be their God. 'He will wipe every tear from their eyes. There will be no more death' or mourning or crying or pain, for the old order of things has passed away."
He who was seated on the throne said,
"I am making everything new!"
REVELATION 21:3–5

My house is my enemy, Lord.

How do I describe the agony of caring for my father-in-law as he died a slow death to Parkinson's disease or the heartache of caring for my mother as I watched Alzheimer's devour her body and mind? I can still see my father-in-law crumpled on the carpet where I found him after his final fall. I still avoid his chair at the table where I struggled to help him swallow, sip, and pull back from the abyss of mental illness.

Five years later, I hear my mother's agonizing cries in the night. I hear her pleas for her mama to come and take her home. I'm awakened by the nightmare of her lifeless body being carried from her room across the hall as paramedics worked to revive her from a diabetic coma.

You're supposed to make all things new, Lord. Can you wash the memories from my home? Will I ever be able to fall asleep without being on guard duty? Will I ever be able to believe I did enough?

Memory is the diary of your life, my child. Erasing memories would void who you were in those moments: my child reflecting my love to the world.

You bore your loved ones' burdens.

You set aside your needs for the cause of love.

You gave when those you loved were too feeble to ask.

You ministered as Jesus' hands and feet. You worshipped me, and I thank you.

I am already making all things new, although it may not seem so to you. Your loved ones are with me, with new bodies free from sickness and earthly limitations. They are celebrating, creating, worshipping, and experiencing inexpressible joy in my presence.

When memories torment you and voices whisper that you're in charge, remind yourself that you rely on me for every breath. I numbered your loved ones' earthly breaths, and I have numbered yours. I am sustaining you every moment, and when your faith is tested, I send the rain that allows you to grow.

Let your faith take root, my child. Endurance strengthens you, and you become perfect and complete through the power of my Spirit.

Hope on the Edge
It's easy for caregivers to believe it's their job to push away death or eradicate illness. If you've taken on these burdens, you've taken on the burden of false guilt. Write those burdens in detail in a letter and take them somewhere significant to you and release them to God.

Read 1 Peter 5:6–7. God asks you to throw your anxiety on him because he loves you. He longs for you to do that and never tires of listening.

Heart Cry

Dear God, help me redeem my painful memories and see them as moments when I ministered comfort and healing in Jesus' name. Thank you that you are sovereign and promise to make good come out of all things, even when I don't understand.

El Olam, Eternal God
Read Ecclesiastes 3:1–14

Most people who've suffered trauma and abuse struggle with a profound sense of loss: lost childhood, lost innocence, lost relationships, lost freedom, lost opportunities, lost hope, and more.

Something inside each of us longs to be anchored to unfixed, eternal, unchanging love we can count on. We want to know we belong. That, no matter what, we can always count on that one person who will never turn away.

El Olam is the Hebrew name for our eternal, unchanging God. *Olam* means forever or never changing. God's plans never change. His character never changes. His unshakable love endures forever.

Written on Our Hearts
No matter what life throws at us, *El Olam*, our eternal God, remains the same. God's love never changes, in spite of our feelings of grief, loss, anger, sorrow, despair, and abandonment.

> 🐚 How does God's unconditional love influence your sense of yourself and the world?

- What do you find comforting about being loved by an eternal, unchanging God?

- God "set eternity in the human heart." In what ways have you longed for permanent, unchanging relationships in your life?

Our eternal God created us for an eternal relationship with him. No breakups. No divorces. No betrayals. Unconditional love and commitment that looks past our faults to our needs. We're all born longing for a home in heaven and God's perfect love, but our messed-up, sin-filled world falls short of delivering.

- Read Psalm 33:11. In spite of how the world fails us, what does God promise?

- Read Psalm 103:13–18. What unchanging qualities of God's character can you depend on?

- Write a letter to God, expressing your feelings about his unchanging love for you. Or create a picture, poem, song, or work of art that depicts the unchanging, eternal love of a perfect Father for his child.

Heart Cry

God, your love and faithfulness endure forever. Help me learn to absorb that truth as my security and help me live as though I can count on your unchanging love for every crisis and every need in every moment of my life.

I accept you.

My Dear Child,
Who condemns you?
Certainly not me.
My son Jesus is the one who died for you—
and more than that—he was raised
and sits at my right hand
and intercedes for you.

—YOUR LOVING FATHER
FROM ROMANS 8:34

God of Safe Places

*Do not judge, or you too will be judged. For in the same way
you judge others, you will be judged, and with the measure you
use, it will be measured to you.*

MATTHEW 7:1–2

It took me decades, Father, to understand that abuse physically changed my brain. I didn't understand that my nightmares and flashbacks, fears, compulsions, obsessions, and even my addictions were linked to responses in my brain that were caused by trauma. That doesn't mean I wasn't responsible for my choices—even the bad ones—but it means my responses made sense.

It was a revelation when I learned that post-traumatic stress disorder is a disease of the physical brain in the same way that diabetes is a disease of one's physical pancreas, and that I don't have to apologize for seeking treatment of an organ in my body that isn't working right. God, you're Lord of my body, soul, and mind when I look for the best possible medical treatment. In fact, you bless me when I'm being a steward of my body.

So when I finally began to understand trauma and made the decision to seek treatment, I expected friends and family to rally around me for one of the scariest decisions of my life.

Some did. But others responded with silence or judgment, as though I'd somehow insulted you, God, by going to the best professionals I could find.

I don't understand why some people seem threatened by mental-health treatment. But I want to thank you for creating a brain that's capable of healing from the atrocities of sin and a fallen world, for creating scientific principles we can access for healing, and for creating medicines and treatments that relieve symptoms. Thank you for my healing.

Give me grace, God, for Christians who sometimes don't understand that those who are ill don't deserve judgment. They need the freedom to speak honestly about their struggles in safe places. And they need the same encouragement to seek professional help for brain illnesses as they do for illnesses from the neck down.

Dear Child,

At the moment when you longed for the supportive arms of loving family and friends, you did not find it. This was a great loss for them, as they gave up the opportunity to share in the blessing of your healing, especially when you extended the invitation for them to participate. They lost out on participating in the gifts you received on your healing journey, and this is their irreplaceable loss.

But, dear daughter, do not focus on others. Do not judge their motives. Leave their hearts to me. You are now responsible to steward the gifts I have given you in your healing. You have insight into the suffering of others. You walk into a room and see through Jesus' eyes. You see pain that is invisible to most people, and you shed light in dark places.

Your journey to healing took you through many valleys so you could become a companion to others and lead them to hope. Look back only to learn from the past and unlock the doors of your future as my Spirit grants you the keys of wisdom.

Hope on the Edge

Have you felt judged in your struggles with trauma and brokenness? What has helped you in the struggle?

It's important to understand that trauma treatment is different from counseling and other forms of treatment. If you suspect you suffer from PTSD, seek out a therapist trained in the most effective treatment for you (see appendix 2 and appendix 3). God blesses your efforts to become well.

Heart Cry

Dear Father, help me to use my painful past in ways that glorify you and give people hope. Help me remember to look back when I can gain wisdom that helps me continue to move forward and bring others along on the journey.

Boiled Frogs

The LORD had said to Abram, "Go from your country, your
people and your father's household to the land I will show you. I
will make you into a great nation, and I will bless you."

GENESIS 12:1–2

Someone once told me if you put a frog in a pot of slowly heating, cold water, the frog won't perceive danger and will cook to death. Its body temperature rises with the water, and it senses that everything is just fine. In my opinion, people who experience abuse often react like frogs in a pot, God. Over time, we numb ourselves to pain, violence, and self-destructive living, and even though the water we're soaking in may be boiling, we tell ourselves we're lucky to be sitting in a spa.

Well, thank you, God, that you came to scoop us up out of the pot to save us from our own stupidity. Sometimes we have to leave people behind. Sometimes we have to leave habits behind. Sometimes we have to leave the things we love and even the people we love behind because those things become our idols and we put them before you.

I'm not talking about husbands deserting their wives for other women or wives leaving their families because things get tough. But I am talking about leaving deadly relationships and creating boundaries that may mean we move to places where we can be safe for the first time or sober for the first time or accountable to godly people who teach us how to grow up and grow in you.

Help us remember, God, that you gave us legs to jump out of boiling water in the first place.

When I called Abram to leave the city of Ur, he did not realize he was living in a boiling pot of sin. Ur was the only town Abram had ever lived in, and Terah was the only father Abram had ever known. But Terah worshipped other gods, and I called Abram to break ties with his family to create a new heritage for future generations. When I called Abram to leave, he didn't know where he was going or how he would get there. He left as an act of total faith in me and abandoned all he had ever known.

When I called Abram, he recognized my voice. He did not confuse me with the false gods he had known all his life. He never doubted I was calling him to new life. My sheep hear my voice and know me. Abram acted on what I revealed to him and obeyed what I asked him to do—one step at a time, one day at a time.

This is my call to all my children. Listen for my voice. I call you to life and to freedom from the sin and death of the world. But you must trust me, and you must be willing to walk away from sin.

Let go.

Turn your life over to me.

Exchange your old life for the new.

Come unto me, my weary child. I am calling you.

Hope on the Edge

What is God asking you to leave behind—to let go of and walk away from so he can move you out of death into new life?

Ask God to give you the wisdom—through his Word, through his people, through the leading of his Spirit—to create accountability and a plan to move you forward. What is one small step you can take today?

Heart Cry

Dear Father, I know I must leave behind the things that are killing me. I commit to jumping out of the pot and fleeing these things. Sometimes they don't feel like choices but like my masters. Give me wisdom to cut chains that bind me, to discern spiritual powers that have a grip on me, and to exercise responsibility for my choices. Lead me to people who can strengthen me for this journey and help me to listen for your direction in every decision.

The Battered Heart

He heals the brokenhearted
and binds up their wounds.
PSALM 147:3 ESV

The first time he hurt me, he shoved me down the stairs. He said it was my fault, God. That I shouldn't have brushed past him without talking and needed to be more careful. I'm not sure what it means to be "more careful" when my slightest mistake causes a man to pin me against the wall with his hands around my throat.

The second time, he blackened my eye when I refused to get in the car with him. I wasn't being a submissive wife, he yelled. It's not reasonable for me to be afraid that he loves driving 110 down the interstate because he's addicted to the adrenaline rush.

He spends thousands of dollars on his hobbies and screams when I spend four bucks on a fast-food lunch. It's all about power, and I'm terrified that the next time he rages I'll be looking down the barrel of one of the guns he cares more for than our own children.

Professionals call him a narcissist, Lord. I left him once. He pleaded that he'd changed, so I gave him a second chance and came back. It was a mistake, and once again I'm being held hostage in the place I long to call home.

I'm trapped and terrified, God. Show me a way out.

Dear One,

I value you as my very own daughter, and I call husbands to cherish and esteem their wives and daughters. You were created to be honored. A husband's role is to love his wife as Christ loves the church—sacrificially and with a love that places your interests above his own. Men are called to reflect this same honor in their regard for all my beloved daughters.

Listen to my wisdom, daughter. Flee danger and find refuge and safety. Do not place yourself at risk because you think you are responsible for someone who abuses you. This is not the "Christian" thing to do, and it is not what I ask you to do. Sacrificing your safety upon the altar of another's sinful ego only feeds the root of their sin. Husbands are responsible before me to love and lead. The submission I call you to in marriage does not empower subservience, relinquish dignity, or bow to abuse.

Jesus got angry and walked away from the hard-hearted, my daughter. He sacrificed himself to redeem sin, not to empower the sinful.

Protect the life I have given you. Protect those I have entrusted to your care. Demonstrate forgiveness, peace, and grace. Allow me to work in you and in the one who betrayed you as you seek safety and healing.

Hope on the Edge

One of the most difficult things we can do is to let go of relationships and walk away. But God does not ask us to submit to abuse and sacrifice our safety. If you are in an abusive relationship, it's important to make a plan. Check out FOCUS Ministries in appendix 3. They offer resources for developing a domestic violence and safety plan, as well as for planning escape routes.

Read 2 Corinthians 1:8–10 (in the Living Bible, if possible). Place your expectations in God, who is our rescuer. What does it mean for you to place your expectations in God again and again?

Heart Cry

Dear God, it is easy to blame myself for the abuse because I've been told it's my fault. I don't see an easy way out. Show me how to be safe and how to protect my loved ones. Lead me to people who can give me wisdom and resources. Help me untangle the knots of my twisted thinking and to stop believing that abuse is what I deserve. Show me your love that will restore my wounded heart.

Skeletons in the Closet

He is so rich in kindness and grace that he purchased our freedom with the blood of his Son and forgave our sins.
EPHESIANS 1:7 NLT

It's time for the sex talk, God. You invented sex, so I'm pretty sure I can be straight with you about the big questions.

Women who've been abused by men often end up telling themselves they hate men and are attracted to women. Or they may throw their bodies at men because their abuser or abusers convinced them that's what they're on earth for. If they've been abused by women, they may try to validate their worth in relationships with men. And if they've been abused by both men and women, they may find sexual relationships with either sex unappealing, or they may convince themselves they're destined to be bisexual or asexual. And if abused women do get married, how do we handle the tension between wanting to be desired and loved and dealing with the fears that come from our sexual triggers?

You created sexual identity, God, but our abusers trampled it in the mud, and we are often left confused, guilt-ridden, shamed, and stripped of healthy relationships.

Do we have the right to be angry, God, about what we lost and what we fear we will never have? And where do we go to talk about pain this intimate, especially when we carry burdens of shame about what was done to us?

You're our Father—my Father. If you care about *everything* in my life, then you care about this.

I'm coming to you, Lord, because I don't know where else to go. Show me who I really am.

Dear Child,

I care deeply about sex because sexual identity lies at the foundation of my plan for the world. I set my plan for man and woman in place at creation, and one of Satan's very first acts was to stir the sexes to war against one another. He expends the totality of his resources attempting to pervert and destroy everything I created, and sex is one of his primary weapons.

Yes, you have a right to be angry, dear daughter, but your anger is a mere shadow of my own for the violence committed against you. I understand why it became difficult for you to trust and why you believed Satan's deception. Abuse slices the spirit open and abandons you in the gutter, where the sewage of lies seeps into your soul.

My Word is clear. I created one man for one woman and one woman for one man. Humanity has always insisted on having its way, however, and choosing what they see as best. And whenever humanity steps out from under my authority, history clearly bears out the devastation in both natural and spiritual consequences.

My grace, mercy, forgiveness, and love extend to every corner of your life, my child. Do change, transformation, and healing come quickly? Seldom. But I am with you on the journey to wholeness in all things. I love you irrevocably and endlessly. Your true identity will always be found in my image and purpose stamped upon your soul.

Hope on the Edge

No one wants to admit their darkest deeds and most shameful secrets, but God knows everything about us and loves us unconditionally. If you've experienced confusion with sexual identity because of abuse, know you're not alone. If you are uncertain where to turn for help, consider visiting FocusontheFamily.com for resources.

God is not a finger-pointing judge but is compassionate, gracious, and forgiving. Your journey to wholeness and healing begins with the first step of coming to him.

Heart Cry

Dear God, sex is one of the hardest things for me to talk about because I feel like my sexual confusion is something no one else can understand. Thank you for loving me. Forgive me for turning my sexual behavior into something it wasn't intended to be and for understanding why I did it. Teach me how to understand sexuality as you created it to be and to see myself as you see me.

The Hardest Thing to Ask

Now all these things are from God, who reconciled us to Himself through Christ and gave us the ministry of reconciliation.

2 CORINTHIANS 5:18 NASB

I didn't know rage was a symptom of trauma, God. After I was sexually assaulted, my parents told me not to talk about it. I could tell they were ashamed I'd been molested. And church leaders told me if I prayed about what had happened, you'd take care of everything.

So I prayed, because I believe that your power and love are big enough for everything.

But slowly my anger turned to rage, and I figured something had to be wrong with my faith. My guilt grew. My anger grew. Ten years later, my children and husband had become the victims of my fury.

Nobody told me my assault was different from other experiences because my brain couldn't process it. For years I felt powerless as the familiar white-hot flare rushed through my veins and I erupted in a screaming tirade. Each time I'd cycle into beating myself up for being a rotten wife and mother.

It took years for me to admit I had a problem and that it had a cause. And it took years for me to find help and get better. Yes, I eventually learned to control my rage. But I needed to ask forgiveness for the devastation I'd caused.

The hardest thing was sitting down with my children and husband and admitting how much I'd hurt them. I didn't mean to hurt them, Lord, but that doesn't erase my responsibility. My "please forgive me" doesn't erase years of pain for my children.

Give me a new heritage, Lord. Teach me to bless the ones I love with my words. Teach me how to look like Jesus in all I do and say. Help me lay down my pride, and give me the heart of a reconciler.

Dear Child,

Sin is the great separator. But your prayer shows the heart of a reconciler—one who is committed to drawing people to me and to destroying works that separate people from me. The key to peace on earth is pleasing me, and that comes by destroying sin through the power of Jesus.

You confessed your sin—to those you wronged and to me. It is gone and eradicated—wiped out. You've begun the work of creating a new legacy. Reconcile people to one another through your words and actions. Draw them to me in the way that you live. Reflect Jesus' love in all you say and do.

Do not make the mistake of living in the past, because those sins are gone. Love your children, and allow me to work in their hearts as you pray for them.

You did the hardest thing of all when you humbled your heart, and your children and generations to come are blessed by your gift and by your changed life. You have broken generational bonds, child.

Listen closely, for the applause of heaven is stirring in the winds about you.

Hope on the Edge

As God's child, you're called to the work of reconciliation and to creating a legacy of hope, peace, and love for your family. In what ways do you fulfill the role of a reconciler in your words and actions? How is God calling you to grow in this role?

Pray about how you can create a legacy of reconciliation in your family. How can you speak peace into broken places? Ask God to give you wisdom and to show you the path to walk as he directs you.

Heart Cry

Give me a new heritage, Lord. Teach me to bless the ones I love with my words. Teach me how to look like Jesus in all I do and say. Help me lay down my pride, and give me the heart of a reconciler.

Building Altars
Read Genesis 35:1–7

An altar is a place designed for worship, praise, or fellowship with God. Altars symbolize God's intervention and protection in our lives. They are places of refuge and comfort, where we're reminded of God's faithfulness in times of trouble.

Written on Our Hearts
Passion and hunger for God's presence are elements in altar building.

- Read 1 Kings 5:5. What factors influenced David's passion for God and his desire to build an altar?

- What things feed your passion for God? What factors in your life have influenced your passion and desire for God?

- Read Psalm 9. In what ways does the psalmist praise God for his faithfulness—even though he has faced suffering and persecution?

❧ Look back on your life. Where have you seen God's faithfulness and protection? Where has he provided shelter and
comfort? Where has he provided mercy and forgiveness?

Consider adapting the following example to build an altar of healing,
commemoration, and worship in your life:

A father and son lived on the west coast of Canada and
loved to go sailing between the mainland and Vancouver
Island. The father had a larger boat and the son a smaller
boat. One day the son's boat capsized in a storm, and he
drowned. His body was never recovered.

As a result, his father had recurring nightmares regarding
the loss of his son. The family had not had the opportunity
to see their loved one buried because the body had not been
found. In his dream, the father sailed to the spot where his
son had perished, leaped over the side of his boat, and dove
to the bottom of the ocean. There he found a treasure chest,
but when he opened it, it was always empty.

At the direction of a Christian friend, the father wrote the
story of his son's death. In detail, he wrote about his feelings
and emotions, including his anger at God and the pain of
losing his son. Then he took a picture of his son, the letter,
and a childhood toy boat to his son's favorite spot overlook-
ing the ocean. There the father dug a hole. He read the letter
to God, told God that he released his son to him, and burned
the letter. He placed the picture and the boat in the hole and
planted his son's favorite tree above them. That place became
the father's altar—a place where he met God and found not
only freedom from his nightmares, but freedom to heal and
move forward, as well.

Building altars is about meeting God in a new way that draws us deeper into his unfailing love. Use your creativity and ask God how you might create an altar to meet him.

Heart Cry

Dear God, I know I need to bury things and burn things in my life and release them to you. Right now, I make this place of prayer an altar where I am meeting you face-to-face. Give me courage to dig holes and set things aflame so that I can die to myself and find healing.

Hope and a Future

Can you redeem this pain, God?

I send gifts that renew you.

My Precious Child,
You will surely forget your trouble,
recalling it only as waters gone by.
Life will be brighter than noonday,
and darkness will become like morning.
You will be secure, because there is hope.

—YOUR LOVING FATHER
FROM JOB 11:16–18

The Man Who Hung the Moon

My God is my rock, in whom I take refuge,
my shield and the horn of my salvation.
He is my stronghold, my refuge and my savior—
from violent people you save me.
I called to the LORD, who is worthy of praise,
and have been saved from my enemies.

2 SAMUEL 22:3–4

When Papa died, I lost my hero—my dashing, charming maternal grandfather who loved people and was unapologetically proud of his family. He was my safe place during the most traumatizing, world-shifting moments in my life. Papa had your heart, God. It didn't matter where I was—lost in a maze of temporary homes-gone-wrong, a humiliating warehouse-like children's group home, or my own chaotic and sometimes scary home—Papa always found me.

Always.

Papa taught me you can be trusted, God, no matter what. He told me you love me more than he ever could and he taught me to really believe "Jesus Loves Me"—the song that became my favorite. He told me you created the moon to be my very own nightlight to help keep me safe in the darkness.

Most of all, he taught me you're my *hope*.

Papa knew I needed hope more than anything. He knew my life

was tough and was going to get tougher. And he knew I'd need love bigger than hate, and truth that shouted louder than lies.

I believed every single word Papa said about you, but you knew Papa's words would never be enough. You came after me yourself and showed me who you are.

I saw glimpses of your love in my papa. But one truly sad thing about life has been realizing that so few people in this world look like you, God.

Your papa loved me so passionately that he captivated people's hearts and stirred a desire for them to know me. He was a special man, but *you* were special to him. He knew you were lost in a world of predators, and even when he hoped you were safe, his heart told him you were not.

So he came for you. Over and over and over again.

The night he left earth and I greeted him in heaven, I heard the question that pounded through your heart: *Papa's gone. Who will come for me now?*

I had already come for you that night, my child. The moon I set in place for you was shining down on you as your papa promised, and I heard every question in your heart.

Do not fear, for I am with you. Do not be dismayed, for I am your God. I will strengthen you and help you. I will uphold you with my righteous right hand.

I bless you with this heritage: that future generations see a passionate love for me in your life, and that they, too, will fall in love with the God who hung the moon.

Hope on the Edge

Who in your life focused your attention on the God who "hung the moon"? How did they help you cling to your faith in God?

How has God grown that faith through the hard moments? "I am with you." Even in the moments when you may not *feel* that truth, in what ways do you still trust it to be true?

Heart Cry

Dear God, help me understand that the God who hung the moon cares about every detail of my life and never leaves me. Help my love grow into an infectious faith-walk that grabs the hearts of everyone I know and love.

Binder of the Broken

The Spirit of the Sovereign LORD is on me,
because the LORD has anointed me
to proclaim good news to the poor.
He has sent me to bind up the brokenhearted,
to proclaim freedom for the captives
and release from darkness for the prisoners.

ISAIAH 61:1

Hi, God.

The day my little brother and I met our "mom," she walked into our lives looking as if she'd stepped off the pages of a fashion magazine. She was wearing a beautiful pantsuit, cool black boots, and a psychedelic paisley silk scarf tired around her gorgeous black hair. And her dimples went on for days.

She sat down in our grandmother's favorite chair in the living room, and we immediately made ourselves comfortable on her lap. She didn't know my brother and I were on a mommy mission, searching for a wife for our dad. I was eight, and my little brother Chris was five. We'd been "interviewing" women for months, and it finally looked as if we had a winner who met our standards. Chris and I silently made the mutual decision to move this beautiful woman to the front of "the mommy who will marry us" line.

I sniffed her. She smelled good, just like a mommy should smell. I remember wanting so badly just to lay my head on her shoulder and wishing she would put her arms around us and tell us everything was going to be all right. But God, I also felt a heavy responsibility to choose the right wife for my father and the right mom for my brothers and sister. After all, I was the oldest and thought it was my decision to make.

Something inside me knew this new mom would give us the things a family needs: physical and emotional safety, consistency, stability, guidance, and discipline. She healed two broken families and made them one. She allowed me to admit I was angry so I could forgive and move on. And she taught eight brothers and sisters with different hurts to like and love each other.

Thank you for hearing the prayers of a child and restoring broken things. And thank you that families don't have to be perfect to understand how love works.

Dear One,

In your lifetime, you will ask me to restore many of the things life cruelly stripped from your hands. Because your heart aches and you feel the void of loss, you will almost always want those things *now.*

The human heart longs for things to be restored because *my* image and *my* heart are reflected in you. I am the source of all that is good, and my children naturally desire completeness and wholeness. Your mom possesses the heart of a restorer and knew how to bind the wounds of children with crushed spirits. Like so many other life-givers I have placed along your path, your mom was my gift and provision for you.

You will not always see the answers to your prayers in the ways you seek, my child. At times, you will grow frustrated, wondering if I'm listening, if I care, or if I'm hard-hearted. The ache will still pound through your heart, and you will be tempted to wonder if I truly love you. But my child, I am present with you always, drawing you to me even in chaos and silence. Often it is more important for you to learn who I am in the silence than to be given the temporary solution you so often seek.

Dear daughter, every day of your life I am restoring and blessing. Learn to trust me in the silence as you soak up new awareness of who I am and share the gifts of restoration you have received with the brokenhearted I will bring to you.

Hope on the Edge

Describe instances when God has used people to restore things in your life.

When has God used silence or asked you to wait in order to teach you more about him? In what ways did you struggle? In what ways has this helped you grow?

Heart Cry

Dear Father, at times silence has felt like indifference, and I've been angry at you. Help me understand that I can learn more about myself and more about you as I learn to trust in your love for me—no matter what. Thank you for being a God with a restoring heart who is working not just to heal me but also to make me like Jesus.

Scattered Jewels

I always thank my God as I remember you in my prayers,
because I hear about your love for all his holy people and your
faith in the Lord Jesus. I pray that your partnership with us in
the faith may be effective in deepening your understanding of
every good thing we share for the sake of Christ. Your love has
given me great joy and encouragement, because you, brother,
have refreshed the hearts of the Lord's people.

PHILEMON 4–7

I don't believe in coincidence. I've witnessed too many miracles and answers to prayer to doubt you're at work in my life, God. When I look back at the most devastating times in my life, I see unmistakable gifts of mercy you placed in my hands.

These jewels of blessing were exactly what I needed in crucial moments: pray-ers, parents, pastors, teachers, and family who provided protection, safety, and nourishment. You handpicked people to surround me when I most needed it, God.

Auntie Susie, who was my safe place.

Auntie Margaret, who was dependable and faithful.

Auntie Hattie, who talked to me about God and prayed for me.

Auntie Connie, who was devoted and giving.

Gwen, who gave me time and taught me how to dance!

Pastor Marilyn Escoto, Tina Escoto, and Leonilda Echevarria, for not letting me go when my life got crazy.

My little sister, Dawn, who may very well be the best person I've ever known.

My mom, Anna, for letting me talk when no one else would. For listening to me without judgment and without shaming me, and for teaching me that being a girl is cool.

My mother, Lil One, for being my strongest advocate for healing and recovery.

Sharalee, the first person who asked me to become part of her family—not because I was thrown at her or the courts asked, but because she wanted me. I have never stopped being amazed.

Therisse (Princess Teri), my beautiful, hilarious, wise and faith-filled friend, who always tells me the truth and loves me unconditionally.

Janet Folger-Porter, my hero, for showing me big faith and how to dream big.

Leah, for putting her money where her heart was.

Pastor Dawn, my sister-friend.

Julianne, my beloved friend and creative, compassionate, tender-hearted prayer warrior.

Shelly, sister of my heart, who always knew where I was inside my head and who became my protector.

God, I'm so grateful for the jewels you gave me, for your grace that covered me, and your mercy that embraces me.

Thank you for sending the exact people we need when life is rough and for being a God who never gives up on us.

My Child,

I sent *many* people into your life when you needed them. Sometimes you saw them and recognized them as jewels, and sometimes you did not. Their prayers have called forth heavenly armies and raised walls of protection around you. They have stood in your path, redirected your steps, and leveled the ground beneath your feet when you were too weary to climb.

Even people you have not recognized as jewels have influenced your life in unseen, positive ways.

People who challenged you.

People who closed doors.

People who told you hard truth.

Unnamed people who prayed.

Unknown people who gave.

Unseen people who saw you when you believed that you were unseen.

Generations who went before you, plowed up parched and cracked soil, and planted seeds.

People who nurtured the faith of those who poured into your life.

I have used them to sift and refine you, to mold and shape you, to teach you difficult but necessary lessons, and to grow you in grace and beauty.

Treasure the jewels, dear one, and learn from them. They are gifts of love from my heart to yours. And know that you, too, are a jewel given to others to reflect my beauty and light into the world and throughout eternity.

Hope on the Edge

Name three of the most influential jewels in your life. What positive role have they played in shaping who you have become?

What influence are you having as a jewel in the lives of others? What has been your greatest positive influence?

Heart Cry

Dear God, thank you for loving me through the arms, words, and actions of friends. Help me be that kind of friend to others. Increase my gratitude for you and your loving care for me and help me not to define your love by the limitations of what I can see. Help me look more like Jesus every day as I learn to reflect his life and his love.

Rehabs and Redemption

It is the LORD who goes before you. He will be with you, he will not leave you or forsake you. Do not fear or be dismayed.

DEUTERONOMY 31:8 ESV

Dear God,

Why is it we think we need to hide our secrets when deep down people are all the same? I hated admitting I was like everyone else who was addicted and needed help. For years I kept telling myself I wasn't one of "those people." I almost died from my self-diagnosed "terminal uniqueness."

I worked hard to hide my inability to cope. I didn't know what it felt like to stand still or rest. I was so very, very tired, and overwhelming sadness drove me to deep denial. I tried to be the fix-it person for everyone's problems. My work ethic and reputation as a valued employee were my proof that I didn't have a problem, even though I was going under. Every day I waited for the moment when I was finally alone and could indulge my secret compulsions—self-abusive rituals—the things far too many people do to cope with their pain.

God, I hated my life and hated who I was. The lies I told myself were so powerful that I couldn't see I was snuffing out my dreams through my own desperate actions. For years I revolved in and out of hospitals and rehabs—drug, alcohol, food—but no matter how good the treatment was, nothing ever came close to breaking down my walls of denial, guilt, and shame.

Except you, God. You never gave up on me. You waited patiently until I came to the end of myself and admitted my total rock-bottom dependency on you. Eventually, I chose to trust you. And on *that* day, for the first time, I experienced true freedom.

Thank you, God, for pursuing me when I thought I could fix myself and told myself I didn't need you. You saw straight through me.

You always do, and you love me anyway. How wonderful is that?

Dear Child,

I smile to hear you say that I see straight through you. Self-deception is such an interesting human characteristic. Most of my children believe I am all-powerful and all-knowing, but in a parallel thought, they attempt to tuck their sins into a corner. They are endlessly capable of believing two contradictory truths at one time. But no matter what they say, their actions demonstrate their true convictions and priorities.

At the same moment you say you believe in my sovereignty, you rush off to fix your messes on your own. But you, child, have discovered this crucial truth: I never stopped running after you when you wandered away, because without me you can do nothing. No matter what horrors you see around you and no matter what pain ravishes your heart, no matter where you flee to find refuge from the devastation of the world, I am with you.

Satan convinced Eve and Adam that they were wise enough to navigate creation without me. Ever since that moment, my children have stubbornly insisted that they are terminally unique and can maneuver through life on their own.

But I never stop pursuing.

Never stop speaking into hearts.

I never give up.

Yes, my child, I saw straight through you. I always do because I love you with a through-and-through love without beginning or end.

Hope on the Edge

God sees right through you and never stops pursuing you. What does this mean to you?

When have you tried to outrun God? Are you still in that place? Tell him about it. He's listening.

Heart Cry

Dearest Father, thank you for coming after me every time I strayed even a step from you. Thank you for seeing where I was heading even before my feet hit the ground. Thank you for pursuing me in my anger and ignorance and rebellion with a love that never runs out. May my love and gratitude drive me further into your heart each moment of my life.

The Hope Bucket

Trust in the LORD with all your heart
and lean not on your own understanding;
in all your ways submit to him,
and he will make your paths straight.

PROVERBS 3:5–6

I didn't know why you whispered Wanda Sanchez's name in my ear that spring day in 2010, God. You wouldn't tell me why I was supposed to call a San Francisco radio producer I'd never met. I'd been on her show a few times, but our only contact had been emails— Wanda passing along show details and the topics her host would be talking to me about in reference to the books I'd written.

For months you nagged me with her name, so I looked her up on Facebook. The only thing I learned there was that she had a heart for inner-city missions. So in what I thought was a flash of brilliance, I decided I'd tell her about my songwriter friend Steve, his organization (Music for the Soul), send her a few sample songs, and convince her to ask him on her show.

Steve had written more than five hundred songs on dozens of issues: suicide, breast cancer, caregiving, eating disorders, pornography, and special needs children. But you handpicked three songs for Wanda that told the story of her life: "Every Single Tear," about how insignificant and invisible we feel in our suffering; "Dead Hearts

Don't Cry," for women ravaged by abuse; and "Renee Is Fourteen," the story of a devastated runaway—which could have been Wanda's biography, right down to her age and the places she traveled on her desperate teenage journey.

You knew that in California a suicidal woman was crying out for help. She was hours away from implementing her suicide plan, and you whispered her name and her story in song to a stranger thousands of miles away.

You had a plan, God, right down to the details of Wanda's healing over the next months. We just had to listen and move our feet.

You came running for Wanda. You come running for all of us. You always do.

Dear Daughter,

Too often my children ask me for help, then turn their attention to the world's din or the sound of their own babble that drowns out my voice. They look for solutions from the wrong people in the wrong places, while ignoring my unchanging Word. They pray for rescue, but often they are not ready to walk into the healing I have prepared for them.

Wanda was ready to do whatever I asked of her. She held out empty hands and admitted her total dependence upon me. She left old places, old friends, old habits, and began a new life. She sought wise counsel and the best available professional care.

Why?

Because she knew I had come for her and she trusted me—no matter how hard the decisions. She rested in my Spirit as she sought help from those who carried her hope until she could carry it for others.

And, my child, when I whispered, you listened and followed the promptings I placed in your heart. You did not take time to count the cost—you recognized my voice and, in faith, left the details to me. I supplied every need for you time and time again. Each and every miracle along Wanda's healing journey attests to my faithfulness.

As you acknowledge me in all your ways, I make your paths straight. I am your Shepherd, the restorer of souls. May you be filled with joy and peace in believing, so that by the power of the Holy Spirit, you abound in hope.

Hope on the Edge

Describe a time in your life when you acknowledged the Lord and he directed you into a new path. How did this affect your life?

What does it mean for you to trust God in your most desperate moment and then move forward? Read Psalm 23 and talk to him about your feelings.

Heart Cry

Thank you that you are a rescuing God and that you even named your son *Jesus* because he saves us from our sins and our troubles. May I become more holy and more like Jesus and not always expect easy deliverance as I walk through painful times and learn to trust your loving heart for me.

Giving Our Suffering to God

Read Genesis 37, 39–45

If we're honest, most of us would admit that we think we're entitled to anger, justice, revenge, and an "even score" when it comes to our abuse. The man who assaulted me when I was nineteen years old was one of the most prolific serial rapists in the Midwest. His victims ranged in age from children to the elderly. And I hung on to my anger and suffering for a lot of years and wondered how God could ever use it for anything good.

The truth is that he does—when we give up control and give our circumstances to him. Giving up control doesn't mean sitting back, twiddling our thumbs, and reacting rather than responding. It doesn't mean that we relinquish the legal resources that are at our disposal for our protection and restoration of what was taken from us. God instituted a system of social justice in the Old Testament that offered protection and a public statement that evil comes with a price.

But God also asks us to acknowledge his sovereignty and to trust him. So how do we do this when the pain of life seems insurmountable?

Written on Our Hearts

- Read the story of Joseph in Genesis chapters 37 and 39–45. It should take you about twenty minutes, but it will be worth the time. Then think about what it would be like to be abandoned by your family—to be unjustly accused—to spend time locked up in a primitive prison cell for years. Describe how you think you may have responded. In what ways would you have justified your anger and revenge?

- How have you justified your own anger and revenge regarding your abuse, abandonment, and the pain of your life?

- The following principles are taken from Joseph's life. Think about each one of them and ask yourself what it would mean to implement these principles.

Joseph gave his suffering to God. This wasn't blind faith but faith that trusted in who Joseph believed God to be. What would it mean for you to give your past and present suffering to God? Pray about real-life steps you might need to take.

Joseph believed God was guiding him through the mess. Joseph interpreted the daily mess within the context of a God with a master plan. How would this perspective change your view of life?

Joseph expected God to redeem his suffering. Joseph invested his time, even when it didn't look like the world around him made sense. He used his "prison experiences" to become a better man. How can you use the "prison" of your circumstances to become a better woman?

Joseph walked in God's grace. He never compromised his values or his faith in God. No matter what happened, he lived a life that served others. He blessed his enemies and sought reconciliation with his abusers. What would this look like for you?

Joseph trusted God in the face of betrayal. Joseph understood that people would betray him, and he didn't get "stuck" in the past. Trusting God was his only hope and security, and he kept his eyes on God. What does it mean for you to keep your eyes on God in your circumstances?

Joseph was confident he would be used. His circumstances looked impossible. But he never stopped expecting God to fulfill his promises. It may not look to you like God can use your circumstances to accomplish anything positive, but he can. Envision the possibilities and ask God to place *his* desires in *your* heart.

Joseph lived in ways that healed and redeemed others. Joseph forgave and blessed his brothers. Forgiveness doesn't mean we have to be involved in the lives of our abusers, but it does mean we release them to God and desire his best for them, including the consequences of their actions. Living redemptively means drawing people to Jesus through our words and actions. What would this look like in your life?

Heart Cry
Father God, help me learn to give my suffering to you—to believe it has a purpose and to use my pain to point people to you. Help me praise you for the blessings I too often look past. Bless the people I'd rather curse and give me a growing grace that brings peace to your world and reconciles people to you through the hope of Jesus.

I bless you with power to release the past.

My Child,
Be strong and courageous.
Do not be afraid;
do not be discouraged,
for I am with you
wherever you go.

—YOUR LOVING FATHER
FROM JOSHUA 1:9

Blood on My Hands

But because of his great love for us, God, who is rich in mercy, made us alive with Christ even when we were dead in transgressions—it is by grace you have been saved.

EPHESIANS 2:4–5

I was twenty-one the day I admitted I was a cold-blooded murderer. The most prolific rapist in our state had gone on a rampage. I was one of his more than forty victims.

And I wanted him dead.

I dreamed of his death. He needed to pay for what he'd done—attacking and raping women, teenagers, little girls. In those days after my world shattered, I told you I wanted him to die, God, and I told you how.

Slowly. Fearfully. Painfully.

He was scum. And certainly *I* was better than a serial rapist. I was outraged. It was years before I admitted that before my attack on that June night I'd never given a passing thought to other women in my community and the world who'd been abused.

But when a rapist crawled through *my* window and into *my* bed, you suddenly became unjust, God. And while a felon named James put a gun to my head that night, in the days that followed, a Christian put a gun to his heart over and over.

It took me years of rotting in hate to understand we're all murderers.

Pull away our veneer of self-righteousness, hit us where it hurts, and hatred spills from all our hearts.

Yet you love us anyway.

You showed me the darkness in my soul so I could be overwhelmed by a love that came for me in spite of who I am. Then you took me to my knees with a love so great it compelled me to forgive the man whose blood flows with the same sinful lust as mine.

Nothing I can ever do will be enough to thank you.

Evil is never only about an act itself. It is about destroying lives that ripple into eternity. The horror that fell on you that June night seeded the spirit of murder into your heart and into future generations. Satan intended the assault on you to destroy your family heritage through your bitterness.

He attempted to blind you with self-righteousness so you would believe you can love me and hate people at the same time.

He used his weapons to make you and future generations see me as a distant, uncaring God who turns my back on suffering.

My child, with pain comes an awakening to what you truly believe—about yourself, about others, about me. Suffering strips away the superficial and exposes the two natures that battle for the soul.

It is true you were born a murderer and a liar on equal level with every human born on this earth except one. My Son—the only human being qualified to wash the blood from your hands, erase the bitterness from your heart, and cancel sin's curse.

I see the gratitude that stirs your soul and draws you to me—not out of duty, but out of love. And nothing is more precious to me.

Hope on the Edge

When have you glimpsed the murderer in your own heart? Were you able to forgive out of gratitude for what you've been forgiven?

Meditate on the saying, "the ground is level at the foot of the cross." What does this mean to you? To choices we must make to forgive? How does it apply to John 3:16?

Heart Cry

Dear Father, I never want to forget that I must put my sinful self to death every day. May I always live out of gratitude and amazement for your incomprehensible love.

Forgiving Bert

Get rid of all bitterness, rage and anger, brawling and slander,
along with every form of malice. Be kind and compassionate
to one another, forgiving each other, just as in
Christ God forgave you.
EPHESIANS 4:31–32

I don't exactly know when or how you did it, God, but you performed a miracle in my life. A part-the-waters, feed-the-five-thousand kind of miracle.

I'm not afraid of Bert anymore—the man who abused and tortured me over and over again when I was a child. For what seemed like forever, he terrified me, even when I became an adult.

If I saw him through a window . . . if I heard his voice . . . if I caught a glimpse of him across a street . . . or worst of all, if I caught a whiff of his favorite cologne, I'd freeze in fear as bile rose in my throat and I'd drift off to a dark, safe place.

Then one day I walked into church and spotted him. I waited for the familiar cold chill of fear on the back of my neck.

I felt nothing.

I waited.

Still nothing.

Moments passed as the realization dawned on me. My fear was gone, as if someone had surgically removed a tumor that had pressed against my heart for decades. With that realization came a second: my burning hatred was gone—replaced by sorrow and pity. That day, my heart released years of anger, and I forgave Bert.

You gave me the gifts of forgiveness and freedom, God. I didn't work for it. You released me from the terror of my past—not because I deserved it but because you love me.

The rest of my life is not long enough to thank you for love that changed my bitter heart.

My Most Precious One,

People often apologize for sin with words, yet never back up those words with actions that demonstrate remorse and repentance. Repentance acknowledges guilt and takes responsibility. A just society requires recompense for evil by demanding that a price be paid that represents the value of what was taken. Unrepentant people refuse to appropriately acknowledge the horror they perpetrate on others with acts of recompense.

My beloved one, you, like so many other precious children, bore the horrible brunt of ruthless sin. And yes, I gave you the gift of forgiveness and freedom from fear for a man without conscience, who never asked your forgiveness. You chose to steward your gift—to share it, to display it to others as a precious possession, and to sow the gift into others' lives. I knew my gift to you would not be squandered. You are the delight of my heart, and when I look at you, I see the face of Jesus smiling back at me saying, "Father, forgive them, for they know not what they do."

Your forgiveness does not free Bert from the consequences of his actions. He will face me in an accounting that will surpass any justice possible on earth, for I alone know the thoughts and intents of his heart. It is a fearful thing for the unrepentant to fall into my hands.

Thank you, daughter, for bearing the image of my Son to the world.

Hope on the Edge

Do you consider yourself more worthy of forgiveness than the worst person who ever hurt you or your loved ones? Are you willing to give the forgiveness God granted to you, or are you still clinging to revenge and bitterness?

Are you angry at God that he would allow such horror to touch your life? Is it difficult for you to see him as loving? Tell him, and let this be your starting point in finding his true heart for you.

Heart Cry

Dear God, thank you for the gift of forgiveness that I don't have to earn or contrive. Thank you that I can trust you to deal with evil and live in freedom from vengeful thinking. Give me opportunities to share your love and goodness and bring people hope.

Choking on the Words

If we confess our sins, he is faithful and just and will forgive us our sins and purify us from all unrighteousness.

1 JOHN 1:9

No matter who I've forgiven in my life, Lord—people who meant to hurt me or people who hurt me out of ignorance—I struggle to forgive myself. I know I don't deserve your forgiveness, and I live every day with guilt for my choices.

Forgiveness for *me*? After everything I've done, God? I know you take sin seriously. So how could you look at my life and not be repulsed by my failures, my rotten choices, and my acts of desperation?

Every day, pictures flash through my memory—things I haven't done, things I failed at doing, people I hurt, things I did that were horrible beyond words.

The pain I inflict on myself only adds to my guilt, even though I've told myself that the cuts and burns and bruises offer me release. But my scars show me that I've added to my agony and released nothing.

Yet in the moments when I've spilled my own blood in denial of your Son's blood shed for me, I still heard you calling my name.

Help me find a way to speak the unspeakable to my own heart: Jesus paid it all. I am truly and completely forgiven.

My precious one, I uphold you every time you fall and lift you when you are bowed down. I blotted out your sins for my sake when you became my child, and I remember them no more.

You're my child, and when I look at you I see the sinless perfection of my Son, Jesus, who paid the price for your sin.

You are *my own*, redeemed and forgiven through the blood of Jesus. Your sins no longer exist. They have been washed clean. Yes, the sin you committed happened, but it has been eradicated. Forgiving yourself is agreeing with me that what Jesus did was enough for you and that you do not have to finish what he started. You are covered in mercy and spared from the eternal consequences of sin that separate those I love from my presence.

When you look at yourself, you see shame. When I look at you, I see beauty. When you look at yourself, you see failure. When I look at you, I see glory. When you look at yourself, you see regret. When I look at you, I see the shining face of my child who has loved and served me, and I say, "Well done."

You will find a way to speak the words when you admit that my grace far surpasses earthly sensibility. Walk out of Satan's prison toward my outstretched hand, away from shame, away from guilt, and into the beauty of your true identity.

Hope on the Edge

In what ways has Satan held you captive in a prison of lies? Imagine a prison with you inside. On each bar, a lie is inscribed. Imagine Jesus opening the door and you walking into freedom as the bars crumble. You stand before him as he crowns you, over and over with glittering crowns of Glory, Dignity, Beauty, Grace, Honor, Purpose, Power, and Authority.

Imagine yourself standing in God's presence, clothed in beauty and crowned with honor as he pronounces the words, "Well done, my beloved daughter." This is who you are. Journal your response.

Heart Cry

Dear God, I admit that grace does not make sense, but today I renounce the lies I've clung to and choose to believe the truth that I'm forgiven and free, no matter how I may feel. I speak the truth: I'm completely forgiven in you. Thank you for forgiveness that's free and not dependent upon anything I have to do. I'm yours, Lord. Use me.

Carry Me

The LORD your God, who is going before you, will fight for
you, as he did for you in Egypt, before your very eyes, and in
the wilderness. There you saw how the LORD your God
carried you, as a father carries his son, all the way
you went until you reached this place.

DEUTERONOMY 1:30–31

Dear God,

For a long time, I was a castle dweller. Not a castle of dreams and rescue and knights in shining armor, but a castle of moats and defensive towers and doors that slam tight. Some people have been hurt so much they try to protect themselves by never trusting again. But what we castle dwellers don't realize is that when we shut ourselves away behind stone walls, we slowly but surely wither, cut off from the world around us.

That was me, God. I protected my heart for so many years until someone came sweeping in on a white horse and convinced me he'd been sent to rescue me—that he was the answer to all my problems sent straight from you. He said all the right things. He even quoted all the right verses.

So I let down the door I'd kept closed to protect myself for so many years, God, and I let him in. I trusted. I gave him my heart. I exposed my vulnerability and opened myself up to be hurt.

I knew it was a risk, but I took the chance.

I gave everything I knew how to give because I believed that's what love does. I picked up his burdens and frustrations along with my own. I didn't know that in striving so hard to love, what I really wanted most was to be loved.

I wasn't prepared for heartbreak and lies. I wasn't prepared to discover how easily my heart shattered like a cheap toy.

But in this very lonely place I've found that trust is not about having the things I believe I need—it's about knowing that you will fulfill my deepest needs when my desires are not met.

So many of my desires are not met right now, God. Teach me to trust you to be everything I need and to heal broken hearts.

Dear Daughter,

Your torn and broken heart is nestled in my hands, and even now I am mending it and breathing new life and purpose into you. Your battered spirit and soul need rest. I am your Shepherd, and I am carrying you in the security of my loving arms. One day at a time, one moment at a time, I call you to find that rest in me. Do not let bitterness, anger, and doubt redirect your heart from mine. I am your only true source of fulfillment.

My child, when you give love, you release the capacity for love to grow within you. When you gave love, you released power that finds its source in Jesus. His love can never run dry and will never fail. Someone betrayed you. This does not mean that others in the world are no longer worthy of your trust. People are imperfect and will fail you in varying degrees throughout your earthly life. Seek wisdom as you find your true source of security in the only unchanging love that exists—me.

You will never live in a world without disappointment and heartbreak, my child.

You can choose to return to your fortress of isolation or to live in the world among other imperfect people like you, empowered by my Spirit flowing through you. I am your God. Earnestly seek me and you will find me. Your soul thirsts for me. Seek to know me at the deepest point of your need, for I am always there, waiting for you. Let the deepest cries of your heart draw you to me so you can come to know and trust me as you have never trusted anyone.

I am who I say I am, and I do what I promise to do. Only I will ever meet the deep longing of your soul. Jesus stands at your heart door, knocking and asking you to let him come into your most private thoughts and to sit with you.

Live in blessing, my child, for I reward those who diligently seek me.

Hope on the Edge

What does your soul "thirst for"? Where has this thirst driven you? In what ways has it driven you to God and away from him?

Meditate on Hebrews 11:6. What has diligently seeking God looked like in your life? What does it look like to diligently seek him and trust him now?

Heart Cry

May I pursue you with even greater passion, God. May my pain be transformed into passion for you. May my hurt be transformed into the confidence that you are my only sure thing in this life and beyond. Thank you for rewarding me when I deserve nothing and for seeking me when I have tried so hard to hide. Thank you for love that never fails.

Empty Arms

*"You do not want to leave too, do you?" Jesus asked the Twelve.
Simon Peter answered him, "Lord, to whom shall we go? You
have the words of eternal life."*

JOHN 6:67–68

Dear God,

I hate baby showers, as horrible as that sounds. I didn't always feel that way.

I used to look forward to the cute decorations, silly games, door prizes, and cake. And of course, the expectant mommy looking as if she'd stuck a basketball under her shirt, happily ripping gift wrap off pastel packages. These things used to make me smile.

Not anymore.

No matter how hard I try to celebrate with my pregnant friends, I wish I were anywhere else. Every moment is excruciating. I'm painfully aware that I make anyone's shower or baby announcement or baby conversation all about me instead of celebrating a precious new life making an entrance into the world.

You know I care about my friends and their babies, God. But you also know the heartache and longing that struck the day of my miscarriage and that have never gone away. My heart hurts and my arms still feel as empty as the day I lost my baby. At night I sometimes awaken and listen for the sounds of my baby, as I lie in the darkness, feeling the ache of empty arms and an empty heart.

I'm broken, Lord, in the deepest place inside my heart and soul. I don't know how to be okay, whether I'm at a baby shower, in church, or walking through a mall.

I know you, God, are the only one who can carry me through this pain and make something beautiful of the biggest loss of my life. Please be close to me in this place of grief as I hold on to you.

My Dearest Daughter,

I was holding you when your own heart stopped beating as you realized something was wrong with your child. I listened to every word you flung toward me—questions borne of the deep sorrow of your heart. I walked beside you as you stumbled from the doctor's office—the finality of your loss confirmed.

I listened as the *whys* poured from your heart day after day.

Could you have done more?

Were you to blame?

What if you'd only . . . ?

I was with you as you agonized over who to tell, what to say, and how to forgive those who approached you with glib answers and shallow spiritualizations.

There is no easy answer for death, my child. If that were so, I would have spared my own Son. We share this pain—the loss of a child—and the promise that life does not end with death. My Son conquered death so your child can be with you for eternity. This truth does not fill your empty arms today, but it is the promise that you will be joined again with your beloved baby forever in a reunion of indescribable joy.

Do not be surprised by the pain in the days ahead. Bring your aching heart to me, no matter how hard or how angry you may feel. As you bring me your pain, it will be infused with hope as you learn more of me.

Cry. Hurt. Know my comfort. I am your hiding place. I alone am God, your refuge and strength.

Hope on the Edge
If you or someone you know has experienced the loss of a child through miscarriage, stillbirth, or infant loss, you may want to visit Mommies with Hope at mommieswithhope.com.

Give yourself permission to grieve and know that God mourns with you. Know that everyone mourns on a different timeline. Consider a GriefShare group as you walk your path of healing.

Heart Cry
Dear Father, my heart is devastated at the loss of my child. Comfort me and give me peace and hope. Help me not to lose heart or become bitter. Heal my body and give me courage to face a new day, confident in your love. Help me believe the truth—that neither I nor my baby did anything to deserve this, and you always act in love. Give me grace to nurture my loving heart as you bring healing for this grief.

WEEKEND FEATURE

Preparing to Release the Past

Read 1 Peter 1:3–9; 4:12–13; 5:6–11

Good friend and author Latayne Scott has written an amazing book titled *The Hinge of Your History: The Phases of Faith* about how we respond when it looks like God is acting in contradiction to his promises.

Much of life can look like this to us—especially when it comes to the pain of our past. God promises to deliver us, yet we wonder where he was the night we were raped.

He promises he will not give us more than we can bear—then we lose our husband, then a grandchild, then a second grandchild, then a second husband—and we sink beneath the weight of grief.

God promises us that he will be our healer, but we watch as our eight-year-old child loses the battle to cancer.

We feel lost, as if our trials are without meaning and that our lives are, perhaps, just a series of random events.

Latayne has walked through grief and brokenness on her own journey. Her husband suffers from a neurological disorder that causes sudden paralysis. Twice he has been taken to the brink of death and left with permanent physical disability.

I encourage you to read Latayne's book to gain her entire perspective on faith in suffering. For the Christian, suffering always provides opportunities for faith building. Like Joseph, we are to learn from the painful and challenging experiences of our lives and allow them to refine us.

Releasing the pain of our past happens when we understand that God moves us through three phases in order to teach us who he is—our loving Father who cares deeply about our every need. Those three phases are

- The promise. God tells us he's faithful, he will be with us, he never leaves us, he always provides. We trust his promises to be true.
- The contradiction. Our faith is tested when trials come and it appears that God has disappeared or isn't faithful to fulfill his promises. Most of life is lived in the contradiction, as we learn to trust in God's character, not what we see from our limited perspective. Releasing the pain of our past often means trusting God's good and loving character, even though it appears that his promises aren't being fulfilled.
- The fulfillment. God shows himself to be faithful to his promises and true to his Word. He is always good and ever faithful.

Written on our Hearts

- Read 1 Peter 4:12–13. We are told to evaluate our experiences, not in terms of how comfortable they make us or how fulfilled they make us feel, but in terms of how much they contribute to the building up of our faith. How have you been able to use your suffering to build your faith? In what ways has this helped you release the past? In what areas are you still learning?

🦋 Read 1 Peter 1:3–5 and Romans 8:28. As Christians, we are shielded by God's power. He filters out the things that could devastate and destroy us. We operate on a different cause-and-effect system than nonbelievers, based on our faith in Jesus. Think about what this means to you personally and write about it.

🦋 Read 1 Peter 1:6–9. These verses make it clear that we will suffer all kinds of grief and trials in this life, but they become of greater worth than gold as they deepen our love for God and fill us with joy. As this happens, how does our perspective on the past begin to change? Have you seen this happen in your life?

Faith always consists of three parts: the promises of God, the contradiction, and the fulfillment. It's easy to see the promises of God and trust him. God always appears to be good, loving, and a giver of all good things in the promise stage. It's when we hit the contradiction that our faith is challenged. Could a good and loving God stand by and allow such terrible things to happen in this world? God appears passive at best and a monster at worst when we don't understand that our faith will always be challenged by contradiction, followed by resolution. During the contradiction phase, when it appears that God has abandoned his promises, we are sheltered and kept. We learn the meaning of hope and perseverance and look forward to the resolution God has promised us.

> 🦋 What does God ask of us during the contradiction phase? Read Romans 12:1–2.

> 🦋 Are you in the "contradiction" phase of a trial right now? Does God look like a passive bystander? Meditate on the passages in 1 Peter and listen for his voice of reassurance.

"God most often calls us to hard, courageous acts that will not bring immediate relief to trials, nor personal advancement, nor comfort and ease."[1] Instead, he asks us to live like Jesus.

> 🦋 What does "living like Jesus" mean for you? What does it mean regarding things you have clung to in your past, things that have stood in the way of moving forward toward resolution in your life?

Look for a piece of art (or create one) that depicts an apparent contradiction that is actually true. If the artwork speaks to you, consider purchasing it and placing it in a place of significance to mark your spiritual journey.

Heart Cry
Father God, it helps me to know that you grow my faith in the contradictions and that you are there with me, filtering out the full consequences and creating good out of evil on my behalf. Give me a

---

1. Latayne C. Scott, *The Hinge of Your History: The Phases of Faith*, 69.

courageous heart, willing to do courageous things for you and not always looking for comfort or ease or relief from my circumstances. Thank you for loving me so much that you have orchestrated circumstances that lovingly pull my eyes away from the here and now to you.

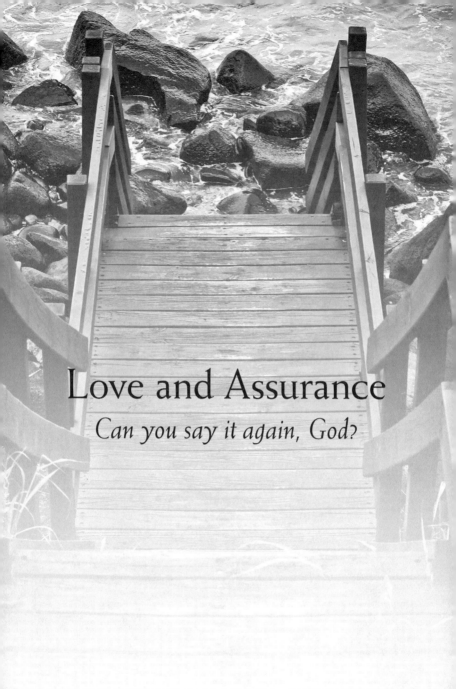

Love and Assurance

Can you say it again, God?

I promise to love you forever.

My Child,
Great is my love toward you.
I want you to know
that my love for you endures forever.

—YOUR LOVING FATHER
FROM PSALM 117:2

Relentless Pursuit

*Suppose one of you has a hundred sheep and loses one of them.
Doesn't he leave the ninety-nine in the open country and go after
the lost sheep until he finds it? And when he finds it, he joyfully
puts it on his shoulders and goes home. Then he calls his friends
and neighbors together and says, "Rejoice with me; I have found
my lost sheep." I tell you that in the same way there will be more
rejoicing in heaven over one sinner who repents than over ninety-
nine righteous persons who do not need to repent.*

LUKE 15:3–7

My Precious Child,

I've watched you as you've wandered the world, carrying the shame
of an outcast. You walk among the crowds, clothed in garments of
self-imposed invisibility, believing you are unwelcome, uninvited, unre-
membered. You strive to cover your imperfections day after day but still
long to be seen and heard and loved as imperfect as you are. Strangers,
trusted friends, even family members have inflicted painful wounds on
your body, soul, mind, and spirit, and you believe you are ruined. The
little girl inside you longs for a rescuer to take on the world, wage war
against the monsters, and pledge his life and honor—just for you.

I am that hero. My relentless love for you drove me to leave heaven,
invade your world, take on human form, and come for you—no matter how hard you ran from me and how lost you felt.

I pursued you each and every time you wandered from my side, following you down dark alleys of despair and into the soul-torn tenements of the lost. I pursued you when you barricaded your heart behind doors of pain and suffering, where you believed you were beyond sight and reach of the light. Even there I sat with you and whispered hope to you in wordless tones. Your soul clung to me, even as you blamed me for the sin I came to heal.

The world has ravaged you with attack upon attack, but I sent the ranks of the heavens to surround you and battle on your behalf, my child. Your earthly eyes cannot see the raging spiritual battle—the powers that I, your Father, the Spirit, and the Son daily unleashed for you in the battle for your soul.

I fight for you. I carry you. And I will not let you go.

When you hid from me, I followed.

When you questioned me, I answered with love.

When you betrayed me, I granted you grace.

When you sinned, I covered your past, present, and future in blood-bought mercy.

I am not rushed, my child. I will always come for you. I am storing good and beautiful things for you in heaven, reshaped from the pain of your earthly life. Jesus came to defeat death so you might live. Call unto me in your weariness, and I will give you rest.

I am already with you. I already came.

Just for you.

Hope on the Edge

When have you been aware of God in pursuit of you? How did you respond?

What does it mean to you to know that God loves you relentlessly—that he will never give up on you or leave you?

Heart Cry

Father God, I've spent so much time believing that you're a God who is standing at a distance watching me and waiting to judge me for my failures. Help me see you as the knight who invaded my world to save me, and the one who never gives up on me. Help me believe the truth of John 3:16, that you *so loved* me with a relentless love, and love me still.

Daddy's Heart

For God so loved the world that he gave his one and only Son,
that whoever believes in him shall not perish but have eternal life.
JOHN 3:16

My Child,

Listen as I open my heart to you. Nothing is more precious to me than time I spend with you, only you.

I am your *Abba* Father—your Daddy. It can be difficult for you to think of me in those terms because earthly fathers are flawed and imperfect. Some daddies are so deeply broken that they hurt even those they love out of their unhealed pain. They may lash out in ignorance or inflict harm because of the evil that was sown into their souls by others. Sometimes they hurt others out of their compulsion to fulfill a false identity someone convinced them was true and real.

But I am your *Abba* Father, the daddy who never turns away and never fails you. I am the father who will never speak a harsh word to you or be disappointed in you. I am the papa who will never forget you or leave you behind. I am the dad who will never lift a hand to harm you.

My every thought and intention for you is motivated by love. No action can originate from me that does not emanate from my essence. As you grow to understand this, you will better understand my love for you infuses all I do because I am the source of love. As your heavenly Father, I can only act toward you in love, because anything less lies outside my character. This truth is your security in a world that defines love as something that can be lost, bought, forgotten, and abandoned.

As your Daddy, I long for you to be near me, to take my hand in trust like a child. I promise to always be waiting for you, always watching for you with anticipation. The things that move your heart move mine . . . no detail or concern of your life escapes my loving care.

Like a proud father, I am delighted when people see my resemblance in you . . . when they look at your face and see my own reflected there, or when they watch your acts of love and see my heart for the world. The deep yearnings that tug at you for goodness, beauty, wholeness, grace, and virtue are your soul-ties and desires for all that is in me. These desires are your heart crying out, *"Abba!* Father!"

You are beautiful, my beloved, my chosen one, and my own. All my desires for you are for your blessing and good. Be blessed with true wisdom, my daughter, and with joy and strength that flow from your security in my love. Know my Word, my child, so that you know my voice. Listen to my still small voice and learn to trust and move at my whisper.

My promises for you are secure. Learn to see and walk in the beautiful things I have planned for you. I have called you to a hope and a future that is hemmed in on all sides by my promises and my love.

Goodness and mercy walk beside you all the days of your life, dear daughter, because I am with you.

I love you,

Your *Abba* Father

Hope on the Edge

God is good—all the time—and his heart for you is perfect love. Write a letter to a broken place in yourself that expresses what God's unconditional love and grace look and feel like. Incorporate Scripture about God's love, and use appendix 6 in the back that states affirmations about God and you.

Choose five of the affirmations to incorporate into your prayers this week as you talk to God. Then journal what he speaks back to you.

Heart Cry

Dear God, you are good, and your goodness toward me endures forever and drives your every motive toward me. Forgive me for judging you by circumstances created by the selfish and sinful actions of others. Thank you for overcoming evil with good and intervening in my life to bring ultimate glory to yourself and to bring purpose out of pain. May I see you more and more as my *Abba* Father, who stoops down to pick me up and hold me close in his arms.

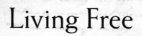

Living Free

The LORD looked down from his sanctuary on high,
from heaven he viewed the earth,
to hear the groans of the prisoners
and release those condemned to death.

PSALM 102:19–20

Dearest Daughter,

Every day, you tell yourself you are a prisoner—trapped and unable to escape.

That your life has no purpose.

That things will never get better.

That you are confined by your bad choices and the life-condemning choices of other people.

That bitterness is as good a choice as any and a better choice than some.

That your real life ended long ago, and the one you are living is a life you do not want.

Those things are lies, daughter.

Geography does not limit my plan for you. The actions of man do not circumvent my purpose for you. Your inability to understand the interplay of time and space, cause and effect, sovereignty and choice does not define eternal reality and destiny.

Before you were conceived in your mother's womb, I crafted a plan and purpose for you. You are still called to fulfill that plan, and every moment of your life marks another opportunity for you to tip the balances of eternal destiny for my kingdom.

Every day of your life is a battle fought on holy ground. Your sacred work begins with your first thought of the day, as I call you to fellowship with me in the intimacy of your spirit. Be still and know that I am God. Be still and know that I am faithful, that I do what I say I will do and complete every good work in you to which I have called you.

You are not a prisoner. No bars exist—within your mind or in the world from which you draw breath—that can prevent you from loving as I call you to love. No law of man can stop you from serving as Jesus served. No power in heaven or hell can separate you from my love.

Where the Spirit of the Lord is, freedom abounds. Do all things to glorify me. Love your neighbor as yourself. Owe no one anything except to love them. Pursue reconciliation. Do not judge. Serve. Know that none of this is possible apart from knowing me and knowing my Son.

Be perfected in my love and walk free, daughter. Freedom is not something to pray for or to struggle to attain. It is your identity— already bought and already owned.

Walk free.

Hope on the Edge
In what ways have you considered yourself to be a prisoner? What things have you missed the most? How has God ministered to your spirit in those losses?

What opportunities have you found to grow in the fruit of the Spirit (love, joy, peace, patience, gentleness, goodness, meekness, temperance) during the prison experiences of your life?

Heart Cry

Dear God, help me to see that you can use me even here and to look for ways to glorify you. My life is not over, no matter what I may see. Use me to bring hope and to change lives. Change me first. May I be so overpowered by your love that I bring reconciliation and peace to those around me and draw them to you.

I Don't Blame You

Therefore, there is now no condemnation for those who are in Christ Jesus, because through Christ Jesus the law of the Spirit who gives life has set you free from the law of sin and death. For what the law was powerless to do because it was weakened by the flesh, God did by sending his own Son in the likeness of sinful flesh to be a sin offering. And so he condemned sin in the flesh.

ROMANS 8:1–3

My Precious Child,

All your life you have struggled against voices that have chided you, blamed you, condemned you, humiliated and shamed you. Too often you believed you were defined by the sin and pain that marked your life. Voices shouted accusations and convinced you that you were worth nothing more than condemnation, mockery, and derision. The maelstrom of pain in your life tore away your identity as my daughter, a joint heir of my promises with Jesus himself. You forgot that when you became my child, Jesus took your rags of shame and clothed you in robes of righteousness.

You struggle to see me as your loving Father who flung the heavens into space for you, because you have devised an image of a god of your own creation, drawn from your limited experiences and knowledge. But I cannot be defined and understood through your earthbound knowledge and experience, my child. I am not the scowling, finger-pointing God you have often imagined me to be. Because of the things that were so tragically taken from you, you sometimes see me as your accuser, tormentor, and critic—as untrustworthy, unsafe, unpredictable, and unloving, like so many people who have marked your life.

But I am not a man. I am Jehovah God, who created the galaxies and the heavens. I am your Savior, who paid the price for your sins so you could have eternal life. I am your best friend, who sits beside you in your deepest suffering. I am your sustainer, who stirred life into your being and controls the mysteries of your body. And I am your Father, who is driven by love and mercy for my children and stoops down to lift you into my arms. My holy character and love defy the confines of your understanding.

I love you. Madly. Extravagantly. I take delight in you—in the sound of your voice, your laughter, and your smile. I take delight in every moment I am with you, in your confidences, and in your love for me. You are my chosen, precious child, and I am your protector and defender until eternity slips off the edge of the horizon.

My heart is for you. It is impossible for me to initiate a thought or action that is not rooted in love for you and driven by my devotion to your best interests.

When voices of blame ring through your thoughts, listen to *my* voice: There is no condemnation for those who are in Christ Jesus. No condemnation, my child. None.

When shame haunts you, speak my words of truth: "Because through Christ Jesus the law of the Spirit who gives life has set you free from the law of sin and death."

When failure haunts you, remember, you're not saved from sin's grip by knowing commands you can't keep, but by the plan I put into effect to save you.

My daughter and adored child, walk with your head held high and your eyes on me. Be blessed with my smile, my approval, my forgiveness, my grace, and my joy as your quiet assurance of my love.

Hope on the Edge

In the moments when you see God as a frowning, judgmental, finger-pointing God, what person does God's voice most sound like to you? In what ways have you formulated your image of God in the image of people in your life?

If you have a relationship with God through his Son, Jesus Christ, your sins are eradicated, and God can only see you with the same sinless perfection that he sees Jesus. Write out a letter or conversation of the things he would say to you about how he feels about you, based on the affirmations found in appendix 6.

Heart Cry

Dear Father, today I claim the freedom that Jesus bought for me. I do not live under your condemnation, and I renounce Satan's false accusations against me. I am your daughter—free and forgiven, and Jesus has freed me from the power of sin and death. You do not blame me, because I'm clean and pure in your sight. Thank you, Father, for freedom from bondage.

Speaking Truth to Your Inner Parts

You desired faithfulness even in the womb;
you taught me wisdom in that secret place.
Cleanse me with hyssop, and I will be clean;
wash me, and I will be whiter than snow.

PSALM 51:6–7

My Dearest Child,

How I love to call you by those words.

My—because you are my own.

Dearest—because you are so precious that I offered the life of my own Son for you.

Child—because I am your *Abba* Papa, your Daddy, and take pure delight in you. But also, my daughter, because it is important for me to speak truth to the child within you.

Humanity has come to believe that age is defined by the number of years one has lived. They celebrate birthdays and call themselves fourteen or twenty-seven or forty-two or sixty-eight. But the truth is that you are the sum total of the days and the hours and the minutes you have lived. Your life encompasses all the ages you have ever been. Although you may be middle-aged, you are still four and fourteen and twenty-four.

Within you, a toddler still whispers fearful thoughts. A child weeps in disappointment. A teenager invites you to be angry with her. Daughter, in each of life's devastating moments, your soul and spirit were bruised, and with the pain came a rush of lies. Some came from the Enemy of your soul. Some came from your efforts to block the pain. Some came from the voices of other people surrounding you in those moments and the days that followed.

Today, those voices still cry out to you, but, my child, I speak truth to those broken places in your inward parts. I am the Alpha and Omega, the beginning and the end, who holds the sum of your time-bound life in my hands. I speak truth, life, and blessing to every devastated and broken part of your life.

I speak to the fearful toddler. I will never leave you or abandon you. I offer you Jesus, the Bread of Life, who satisfies every hunger and lifts you up to carry you in loving arms.

I speak to the child weeping in disappointment. I never forget you, and even the smallest detail of your life is my highest priority. You are so important to me that I have written your name on my hands because my every action reflects my care for you.

I speak to the angry teenager. I see you and love you for who you are. In spite of your foot-stomping and head-tossing, I will never reject you.

I speak to the broken woman. I will never betray your trust or sacrifice your good. I am your comfort and your strong tower.

My child, I speak life and truth and healing and grace to the inward parts of you that ache to be loved and embraced. My voice is not the voice of a critic or judge but the voice of a loving father calling you into his arms.

My dearest child. Let these words saturate the core of your soul and spirit. Let them cleanse you from false identities as you embrace who you are as the daughter of my heart.

Hope on the Edge

What "inward parts" of you cry out in their brokenness? What lies do they speak? What truth does God speak to those broken places?

"My dear child." Listen as God speaks those words to you. What do they mean to you?

Heart Cry

Dearest *Abba* Father, help me see myself as your dear child. Let that truth change the way I talk to myself and about myself, and give me new freedom. Free me from guilt and shame as I learn to recognize your grace for all of me.

Counting on God's Unfailing Love

Read Psalm 36:5–7

The world around us is changing. Technology is moving faster than most of us can keep up with it. Scientists and other smart people say that the earth's systems are continually changing from order to disorder. Overnight, governments topple, and new ones pop up. Day after day, without fail, the news across the globe is the same: change is a part of everyday life in our world.

Change can be frightening and bring a sense of threat, especially when we don't know who's in control and if they care about us. Often our sense of security collapses when life falls apart and we become sick, lose a loved one, mismanage our money, or lose our material possessions. Life and loss bring change that can be unsettling, no matter how inevitable the circumstances may seem.

So what can we count on? Where can we find a source of security in a world that holds no guarantees? Who can we count on when even friends and family fail us?

The world holds only one source of hope: God, who will never cease to exist, cease to pursue us, or stop loving us. And he is so much more than eternal. He is absolutely unchanging, and because he is unchanging, his love for us can never fail.

Ever.

The reason is simple—God simply cannot change.

His love never fails.

Written on Our Hearts

🐟 Have you ever been in a situation when circumstances and people seemed shaky and undependable? In what ways were people unable to "come through" for you? How did you respond?

🐟 Write about a time when God demonstrated unfailing love for you that didn't change and didn't give up. What did this mean to you?

🐟 Read Psalm 36:5–7. How are love and faithfulness related? How have they been connected in your life? In what ways have you seen God's faithfulness at work on your behalf?

🐟 Still in Psalm 36:5–7, how are love and righteousness related? How have they been connected in your life? In what ways have you seen God's righteousness at work on your behalf?

- What does it mean to "take refuge in the shadow" of a love that never fails? Have you found this refuge in God? In what ways do you desire to experience it in greater abundance?

- Write out Psalm 36:5–7 and carry it with you this week. When you feel discouraged, pray these verses to God. Write about how this act of praise influences your thinking.

Heart Cry

Thank you, God, that you are the one sure thing in my life that never changes and that I can always count on your love—no matter what. Father, when I begin to feel as if I'm coming unglued and things feel shaky and uncertain, I know your love is always there for me and I can run to you for refuge.

I promise you a hope and a future.

I am the Lord your God
and I am with you.
I am the Mighty Warrior
who saves you.
I take great delight in you
and rejoice over you with singing.

—YOUR FATHER GOD
FROM ZEPHANIAH 3:17

Unthinkable Grief, Unfathomable Hope

*No, we declare God's wisdom, a mystery that has been hidden
and that God destined for our glory before time began. None of
the rulers of this age understood it, for if they had, they would
not have crucified the Lord of glory. However, as it is written:*
"What no eye has seen,
what no ear has heard,
and what no human mind has conceived"—
the things God has prepared for those who love him.

1 CORINTHIANS 2:7–9

My Dearest Child,

I have promised you an eternal home in heaven with me, and I want you to better understand that heaven is what you have been looking for all your life: ultimate fulfillment. Heaven is about me.

The other day you discovered a musical artist who captured your heart. You played his song over and over, then shared it with your best friends. The next day you played his music again.

And again.

And again.

Why? Because his music satisfied something deep within you.

The satisfaction that floods through you as you listen to a song or sip a strawberry milkshake or watch the evening sun slip over the horizon is rooted in me. I am the source of all earthly satisfactions and the giver of all good gifts. My gifts include the bounty of sumptuous foods, the glories of nature, the magnificence of music and artistic expression, and limitless blessings for your body, soul, and spirit.

All joy emanates from me. All satisfactions find their source in me. All peace and significance point to me and find their fulfillment in me. Earth offers you secondary glimpses of me, like a clouded mirror reflecting my image. Now you see me only as a reflection in a mirror. In heaven, you will see me face-to-face and will fully know me. In that moment, you will fully come to life for the very first time, as you look into my face.

The desires that drive you every day of your life and that long for satisfaction will finally be realized in me in heaven. The longings of your heart will be fulfilled in exponential ways impossible for you to conceive. No longer will you be tempted to make idols out of secondary, temporal provisions and worship the gifts instead of the giver. In heaven you will finally be joined with me—the giver of all gifts.

In heaven, your heart will explode in gratitude and praise, and every gift, talent, passion, and ability I knit into your being will burst into fullness. This is why heaven is your home, my dear one. And this is your comfort in grief for those you have lost to death and who are here with me now.

Dear one, until that day when I gather you in my arms, do not make idols out of my good gifts. Use them as the blessings I intended—to draw you to me and to remind you of my great love for you. Glorify me by finding your satisfaction in me.

Do not make the mistake of separating joy from me—the source of all joy. Heaven is your true and only home, where you will know ultimate joy in my presence. I have made every provision for you beyond your wildest dreams, my beloved. And your loved ones who are with me no longer enjoy mere secondary joys. They are exploring limitless expressions of ultimate joy in my presence.

I bless you, my daughter. I keep you, my daughter. I make my face to shine upon you. I bless you with grace and peace until that day when you see my face and all else becomes clear.

Hope on the Edge

Think about a favorite thing that you love doing over and over because it satisfies you. In what ways could you be tempted to make this thing an idol? How can you use this to point you to God as the provider of all good things?

We sometimes fear heaven because we think it will be a place that will be boring. How does thinking of it as a place that provides ultimate satisfaction change your view of heaven? Consider reading Randy Alcorn's book *Heaven* on this subject.

Heart Cry

Dear Father, help me live with a view of heaven as my home and you as the giver of every good gift in my life. Help me grieve with hope and a vision of heaven as the ultimate home for my loved ones. Make heaven more a part of my life every day as I live with greater satisfaction and purpose every day.

Face Time

*But the Pharisees and the teachers of the law were furious and
began to discuss with one another what they might do to Jesus.
One of those days Jesus went out to a mountainside to pray, and
spent the night praying to God.*

LUKE 6:11–12

Dear One,

Day after day I watch you struggle. You feel as if you are alone, but
I am here, my child, whispering words of love.

My voice whispers to you in the rustle of the wind and the song
of the bird: "I am with you. I am here. I love you. Trust my power
and love that encompass and overshadow all you see and could ever
understand." I created the beauty of nature for you. Every time your
heart is drawn to beauty, it is crying out to me.

Look at the goodness in people around you and know that you are
created in my image. You are not the product of evolutionary chance,
but a unique creation that reflects my eternal purposes. Know that
I am working out a plan that supersedes what you see and that will
redeem even the most horrific pain for my glory.

Look at the sinfulness in the world around you and in yourself and
know that my love compelled me to invade the world on your behalf.
My love for my children is driven by an endless supply. I will never
leave you or forsake you. I fight for you and with you in your battles.

Look at the world around you and the scope of history and see the battle raging between good and evil that is leading to the final redemption from sin. For every instant in history, my child, my plan has been unfolding, and you play an integral part in my purposes for eternity.

Most of all, child, I desire time alone with you, face-to-face. I long for you to open my love letter to you—my Word—and to sit with me. There I have poured out the promises of my heart—just for you. Stories of old friends who also suffered, doubted, failed, and overcame. Songs of doubt and discouragement. The epic battle that has waged for the souls of every man, woman, and child—and the final scenes that are yet to be played out. There you will find something new every day—something just for *you*, written from my heart to yours.

I long to meet you in prayer, my child, as you express your heart to me. I created you so we could communicate at any moment and I can be with you in the intimacy of your thoughts through the power of my Spirit. That aspect of intimate communication was created for my children alone, so we can talk freely about anything and everything, any time of the day or night.

Do not be anxious about anything, my child. Bring everything to me in prayer—your requests and supplications, your thanks, your questions, your doubts, your anger and frustrations—and make them known to me as you learn to trust my goodness and love for you. As you come to know me more, my peace will surpass your human understanding—the peace that guards your heart and mind in Christ Jesus.

You are loved, my daughter, and I long to hear your voice.

Hope on the Edge

How does it change your thinking to know God created your self-talk to be a unique place to meet with you and talk? Think about how you might increase your conversation with God throughout the day and how it might change your awareness of his presence.

Describe your prayer life. In what ways would you like to feel closer to God?

Heart Cry

Dear Father, help me see you wherever I look and be reminded that you are with me and caring for me. Help me remember that you're just a thought away and waiting to talk to me—about anything and everything. Help me learn to listen in to my self-talk and meet you there as I become more aware of the lies that I speak to myself and replace them with your truth. And God, help me not just love you more, but fall in love with you more.

You Are Not Forgotten

Can a mother forget the baby at her breast
and have no compassion on the child she has borne?
Though she may forget,
I will not forget you!

ISAIAH 49:15

My Precious Child,

Listen to my words and hear my heart. Since the beginning of time, long before you were even conceived, I loved you completely with a love that is pure and everlasting. You were then, and you are now, the apple of my eye, and I delight in you. You are my precious child. You belong to me.

My daughter, I know the challenges you have faced and the victories you have celebrated. I know the things that make you smile with delight and joy, but I also see the things that have diminished and wounded you.

I know the things you fear most—things that would plunder and destroy your life and the lives of those you love. I have heard your cries, and I see the wounds of your soul and hold your broken heart close to mine. I see your hurt, my beloved. Trust me. I offer you a refuge for the deepest heartaches of your soul, renewing and refreshing those dry and barren places.

Rest in me, my daughter. I know exactly where you are today. You are not forgotten. You are mine—wonderfully and uniquely created by me for a specific purpose—and I find great pleasure in you. You are forever in my heart and in my thoughts. I whisper your name without ceasing, and you make my heart smile.

I sense your panic and your pain. Cling to the truth of my love, my cherished one.

Speak it, claim it, live it, and never forget: my love for you is everlasting and unconditional, my beloved, unforgettable daughter.

Hope on the Edge

How has God created you uniquely? What desires and aspirations has he placed in your heart?

God takes indescribable joy in you. What things about you bring him joy—not things that you do, but things about who you *are*?

Heart Cry

Dear God, it's hard for me to believe that you care about my problems, but you are God and you cannot lie. You are faithful to your word, and you loved me enough to sacrifice your own Son. Help me remember that every moment of the day and night your love pressed me into your thoughts. Grow joy and confidence in me to live in that love.

Mine for Eternity

*Then the LORD God formed a man from the dust of the ground
and breathed into his nostrils the breath of life, and the man
became a living being.*

GENESIS 2:7

My Precious Child,

In the beginning of creation, I spoke the world into being with the power of my word, and your story was set into motion. But even before I spoke the words "Let there be light," I knew you.

I knew everything about you—who you are in this moment in time and who you will become.

I knew the music you would love and the food you would hate.

I knew the struggles you would face in third grade and the mean girls who made you feel like you didn't belong when you were thirteen.

I knew your unformed thoughts in the womb and your squeals of joy in your childhood.

I knew every sorrow and struggle you would face in life and the characteristics of your personality that would steer your choices in those battles.

I know you better than you know yourself because I formed you as my unique creation. And before the dawn of time, I chose you, my child, as my own. You are my special creation—uniquely designed and crafted in the details of your personality, your body, and your spirit. I created you to fulfill a unique purpose in the universe and in history—a purpose only you can fulfill.

Know, my daughter, that your imperfections do not somehow override or redirect my plans for you or the world. My sovereignty encompasses who you are and every willful or unintentional act carried out by humanity. Because of this, you can live with confidence, in spite of the pain you may feel or the circumstances you may see surrounding you. My Holy Spirit within you even at this moment is working to guide you, equip you, and develop and shape your identity. This will come as you walk the journey of your life, my child, but my indwelling presence will be with you for every step and every breath.

Because of my Spirit in you, you can know peace, even in chaos and pain. I bless you with my peace that passes understanding, my child. I bless you with eternal security and eternal provisions that rescue you from the Enemy's snares. When I set my plan in motion for you, I did so because I created you to be mine for eternity. Nothing can keep you from my love, and I moved heaven and earth out of my great love for you.

When I crafted the universe, I took the time to create only one thing by hand and breathe my own breath into its being—my children. The world will tell you that you are nothing special, but they speak lies. Your being declares my glory to the world, and I have set you on earth to proclaim my handiwork to the universe.

You are my hand-signed masterpiece, my daughter. My fingerprints are on your life, and I declare you my own, my chosen one, mine forever, and eternally loved.

Hope on the Edge

God knows you better than you know yourself, with all your flaws and imperfections, yet he loves you unconditionally and promises never to abandon you. Have you struggled to believe this? How does truly believing this influence the way you think and live?

Meditate on John 3:16. Write out what the words "so loved" mean to you.

Heart Cry

Dear God, it blows my mind to think that you loved me even before creation and designed a way to make me yours for eternity. Help me live with a big-picture view of your love and of my life that lifts me above my everyday circumstances and trusts you to make sense of things that make no sense to me. Help me rest in knowing that I don't need answers as much as I need to know you.

Leaving and Letting

*Peace I leave with you; my peace I give you. I do not give
to you as the world gives. Do not let your hearts be troubled
and do not be afraid.*

JOHN 14:27

Dear Child,

Everyone in the world is searching for peace, longing to rest in a place where they feel accepted, loved, and safe from threats. One thing is certain: peace will never be found if you are hoping for security in the circumstances *outside* you. The world will always be filled with conflict and turmoil. You will always be surrounded by haters, abusers, antagonists, and those whose irresponsibility collide with your need. The world will always be unfair and unjust, and if it does not disappoint you, it will disappoint the people you love.

Humanity seeks peace because they seek me, the essence, source, and substance of peace. To admit the possibility of peace is to acknowledge my existence. To know true peace is to know me.

I give peace as a gift of my Spirit to my children—not an absence of conflict in the world, but a deep, irrevocable awareness of my presence. This peace enables you to embrace your problems and view them as challenges and opportunities for growing in faith and in your relationship with me. It is the lock that opens the door to new facets of my character and love for you. The peace I give to you passes all understanding. It is not simply calm in a storm or lack of fear. It is the ability to embrace trials with the confidence that I can use even the deepest suffering for your good.

You will face moments when circumstances suggest that I have abandoned you. Life will not make sense, and you will be tempted to create answers for yourself and devise a god in your own image.

Leave the tension of the contradiction in my hands. Let go and allow me to be God. My promises will never fail. I work all things together for good for those who love me. I have called you because I have a purpose for you, and my plans never fail. No device of man or Satan can overthrow the plan I have set in place for you.

The peace I give to you I do not offer to the world. But you are my own, and I am working in all things to bring precisely the right outcome at the right time for your good and my glory.

Be blessed with my security and intervention. Know my favor and freedom from anxiety and fear. Bring my peace to the world, my child, as you drink deeply of the joy I place in you.

Hope on the Edge
It often feels like life is chaos and, if there ever was a plan, it went off-track somewhere. When has it been difficult for you to trust that God still has a plan for your life? When have you struggled most with peace?

It can be difficult for those who struggle with PTSD to feel God's presence. But emotions do not define reality. Meditate on the following verses: Isaiah 54:10; Matthew 11:28–30; John 16:33. What is God saying to you about his peace?

Heart Cry
Dear God, sometimes I don't *feel* at peace about my life, but I claim peace as the reality of who you are and your unchanging character.

I stake my life on your promises and your love for me, and I move forward in confidence, claiming my identity in you. Increase my confidence to believe beyond what I can see, and give me courage and wisdom to bring peace in the world around me.

Remaining Rooted in Hope and Truth

Read Philippians 4:4–9

Sometimes just getting out of bed in the morning can feel over-whelming because we've lost hope.

Not too many years ago, a loved one dear to my heart returned from overseas devastated by post-traumatic stress disorder. Even the small-est tasks of daily life were almost impossible for her. It broke my heart to hear the discouragement in her voice as we talked over the phone. But over the weeks and months, friends surrounded her. She found a traumatologist who knew how to deal with what she'd experienced. And gradually the symptoms of PTSD diminished.

One day as we talked on the phone, I asked her how she was manag-ing to cope.

"Sometimes just getting up and doing the everyday things reminds me that life can be good again."

Written on Our Hearts

God has given us simple but profound weapons to focus our hearts and minds on truth and hope. In the Bible, we see the power of object lessons to represent inward expressions of faith.

For instance, God used the ark of the covenant and the tabernacle to symbolize his presence with the children of Israel. He used manna to symbolize his unfailing provision and faithfulness. And he used a dove to embody or represent the presence of the Holy Spirit when Jesus was baptized (Matthew 3:16). Because our earth-bound bodies filter knowledge through our senses, we sometimes grasp spiritual concepts more clearly when they are represented in a physical form.

> Read Philippians 4:8–9. Answer each of these questions— from God's perspective of you:
>
> What is true about you?
>
> What is noble about you?
>
> What things are good and right about you—not the things you have done, but things that mark your integrity and character?
>
> What things are pure about you?
>
> What is lovely about you?
>
> What is admirable about you?
>
> What is excellent and praiseworthy about you?
>
> After you have answered each question, *think on these things.* These are the true things God believes about you. This is the inner voice of truth God speaks to you through the power of the Holy Spirit and that should imprint your self-talk and your actions.

🐚 The Philippians 4:8 Project. Create a visual representation of the truth of your identity. Let it take a form that represents your creativity and personality. These are just a few suggestions:

- Plant a garden. Use it for meditation and prayer, and let the various flowers, shrubs, plantings, and other creative aspects represent the elements of your true identity.
- Transform an old trunk. Paint it or decorate it and fill it with Philippians 4:8 objects that represent your true identity.
- Create a mosaic table. Purchase inexpensive pottery plates in different colors that represent your false, former identity. Break them, then reshape them into a mosaic table. Imbed Philippians 4:8 or another verse that represents your true identity.
- Repurpose an old window. Give it a "shabby chic" look or paint it. Behind the window, place pictures, words, verses, and other images that represent your true identity.
- Paint a picture, write a song, create a photo collage, or use any other form of artistic expression that represents your true identity as a beloved daughter of the one true God— chosen, cherished, and eternally loved.

Heart Cry

May my life be a love letter to you, Father God, written with a steady hand as I live with growing passion for the things of your heart.

PTSD 101

Many people associate the term *post-traumatic stress disorder* with the mental health challenges faced by those in the military when they return from combat. But according to the Sidran Institute for Traumatic Stress Advocacy and Education, *approximately 8* percent *of all adults will develop post-traumatic stress disorder during their lifetime.*[1]

What is post-traumatic stress disorder? Mayo Clinic defines post-traumatic stress disorder as a mental health condition that is triggered by a terrifying event. Symptoms may include flashbacks, nightmares, severe anxiety, as well as uncontrollable thoughts about the events, and triggers related to the event that cause flashbacks and memories.

What makes an event traumatic? Psychological trauma occurs when a person's *ability to cope* is overwhelmed by a highly stressful experience and an individual perceives a threat to his or her own life or the life of someone else. Circumstances can include betrayal, neglect, entrapment, abandonment, abuse of power, physical abuse, emotional abuse, helplessness, pain, confusion, or loss.

---

1. "Post Traumatic Stress Disorder Fact Sheet," Sidran Institute, accessed December 6, 2013, www.sidran.org/sub.cfm?contentID=66& sectioned=4.

Trauma can be a response to a single event such as a natural disaster or automobile accident. It can also be a response to loss from a terminated relationship such as through adoption (when a child feels given away or abandoned by the biological mother or when a biological mother struggles with having given up her child), divorce, or death. And trauma can be a response to ongoing acts such as physical, sexual, and emotional abuse. The more an individual believes he or she is endangered, the more traumatized that person will be by their circumstances.

Why do people respond differently to trauma? Many factors play a role in the way people respond to trauma. These factors include whether or not the trauma was a single event or ongoing over a prolonged period of time; whether the individual experienced other traumas in their life; whether the experience occurred in childhood or adulthood; whether the trauma came at the hands of a stranger or a trusted family member or caregiver; whether the person experiencing the trauma had a strong support system; the mental health of the individual at the time of the trauma, as well as other factors. For this reason, an event could occur and cause traumatic symptoms for some individuals and not others.

What are the symptoms of post-traumatic stress disorder? Symptoms of PTSD include

1. **Reexperiencing.** People with PTSD often feel like they're experiencing their trauma over and over again. This is sometimes called a flashback, and it's different from a nightmare because the person relives the traumatic experience.
2. **Avoidance.** In order to avoid the triggers that cause them to

reexperience the trauma, they sometimes "zone out," go numb, or dissociate. People with PTSD also use drugs, alcohol, and self-abusing behaviors to control and avoid their pain.

3. **Hypervigilance.** People with PTSD are often jumpy, easily startled, and may have *insomnia, nightmares,* and *sleep disturbances.* They often feel they have to be on guard and are *hypervigilant.* They may have *obsessive-compulsive disorder* related to traumatic experiences (for instance, fear of bugs if they were locked in bug-infested spaces). They are sensitive to *triggers* that are associated with their trauma. These triggers can include sights, sounds, smells, sensations, and can be things the individual does not consciously remember.

What kinds of things can cause PTSD?

Witnessing or experiencing

- Physical, emotional, or sexual abuse
- An accident or violent crime
- Life-threatening and emotionally threatening situations (In addition to military personnel, this is also common among those with careers in law enforcement, firefighting, prison and judicial work, and first responders.)

Experiencing

- Abandonment or neglect
- The death of a loved one
- Natural disaster
- War
- Adoption
- Medical trauma (This can include various medical traumas

and experiences, even as a preverbal child, including but not limited to: cancer, chemotherapy, cardiac problems, childbirth, in utero and neonatal experiences, spinal surgery procedures, and "locked-in" medical trauma such as stroke, paralysis, or Guillain-Barre Syndrome.)

What do people with PTSD feel like? People with PTSD often feel *guilty* about their inability to control their thoughts or behaviors, such as responses to triggers. They also may feel guilty about behaviors that are often linked to the symptoms of PTSD: addictions, obsessive-compulsive behaviors, self-abuse, eating disorders, and a negative self-image. And they often feel like "second-class" Christians and a disappointment to God, family, and friends.

People with PTSD often feel *isolated* from others. They tend to hide how they really feel, as well as the things they do, fearing judgment from those who don't understand their illness. They also feel the isolation that comes from living with phobias, and they often separate themselves from others and go into "hiding."

People with PTSD also often feel *depressed* and may struggle with *suicidal thoughts*, which are part of their illness. They may feel guilty for seeking medication or counseling and be reluctant to seek the help of a physician. Or they may have sought counseling or help and found it to be ineffective, which adds to the cycle of depression.

The good news is that PTSD can be treated. Thousands of people have found help and healing from their symptoms. But healing begins with admitting you need help and assessing your level of need. For further information, consult with your health care provider or therapist, or begin by taking a PTSD assessment test (see appendix 2).

Common Therapy Approaches for PTSD

Cognitive Behavior Therapy is based on the premise that changing the way we think changes the way we behave.

EMDR (Eye Movement Desensitization and Reprocessing) stimulates the information processing system so that memories in the past are "digested" and can be filed as memories that have taken place in the past.

Talk Therapy utilizes insight, persuasion, suggestion, reassurance, and instruction to help survivors cope with and overcome symptoms.

Exposure Therapy operates on the principle that we get used to things that are just annoying and not truly dangerous.

The **Instinctual Trauma Response Model** helps clients process their trauma narratively using a "parts" approach so that they can gain a perspective that allows them to replace the mythology that they are hopelessly endangered. Treatment is completed in five to ten days.

What can I do if I feel triggered? (Basic Grounding Skills)

- Look around the room. Identify and name some of the things that you see. Becoming more aware of where you are now helps you fight off being sucked back into the past.
- Rub the palms of your hands together. Pay attention to the sensation of warmth this creates in your hands. This trick makes you feel calmer by changing how your hands feel.
- Listen to music. Choose soothing, calming music that will relax you. Or if you prefer, choose music you can sing along to that reminds you of a pleasant memory.

- Do any kind of physical activity that your physical ability allows. Focus on how it makes your body feel. Muscle tension will diminish as you do this, and you will feel calmer.
- Spend time with your pet. Stroke their fur, talk with them, play with them, or hug them.
- Carry a small, meaningful object in your pocket that reminds you of the present. Touch it to remind yourself that you are in the present and you are safe.
- Look at your cell phone or a clock. Remind yourself that this is today, and tell the frightened part of you that they are no longer in danger.

A Day in the Life

The following blog post, adapted from a posting from Jim LaPierre, LCSW, CCS, is a vivid description of what it's like to live with PTSD.[2]

Four a.m. is her witching hour. She wakes each morning with adrenaline coursing through her veins. Her heartbeat hammers, and every muscle in her body is tense. She's in fight or flight mode, but there's no one to fight and nowhere to run.

The first thirty seconds feels like half an hour. It's the time in between sleep and waking. What's real? What isn't?

It's much worse than a bad dream. It. Feels. Like. It. Just. Happened. Again.

---

2. Jim LaPierre, "Waking Up Scared (Healing, PTSD & Sexual Abuse)," Recovery Rocks blog, August 3, 2013. Used with permission. Jim can be found at http://recoveryrocks.bangordailynews.com.

The tears come, but she fights them. She checks the sheets, but they're clean. She sits on the side of the bed, rocking back and forth, but it's a little too fast to bring comfort.

"Breathe!" Can't get enough oxygen. Hyperventilating is terrifying. Head pounding. Need light. Need air. Must get out of this room.

She starts the coffee. No chance of going back to sleep now. Go to the bathroom but turn away from the medicine cabinet mirror. Cold water on her face stings but feels real. Still avoiding the mirror, can't stand the image there. She needs a shower but it doesn't feel okay to do that yet.

Settle in with some reading—daily affirmations. Get centered. Prayers are sent but feel futile. She never got the hang of meditation. It just gets her stuck in her head. A song on Pandora grabs her attention:

I'm still alive but I'm barely breathing. Just praying to a God that I don't believe in.

Make plans for the day. Staying busy helps. Make lists. Combine them with yesterday's lists. Sun's coming up. Therapy today. Have to take a shower. Fear. Self-loathing. Shame.

Scalding hot water. Pain. Scrubbing way too hard. Still can't remove the feeling of being dirty. "You know that it's not on your skin. It's burned on your memory. It's a feeling of shame based on what was done to you. It's not your fault. Please cool off the water. It's hurting you."

She doesn't know that others struggle with these feelings, too. I've tried to be gentle but direct with her in therapy. "You're naked and wet in an enclosed area with nowhere to run or hide when you shower. You close your eyes to keep the shampoo out. You can't hear what's going on in the rest of the house. You feel physically vulnerable. It makes sense that you're scared."

I want to help her stop feeling like she's crazy, like she's the only one who struggles with these feelings.

We talk about how she copes, how she sees herself, how she struggles to have self-control. She confesses what she sees as sin.

"I feel like a little girl a lot of the time." She finds it hard to believe that I have known a lot of adults who feel like children.

I ask her to recall how she described feeling broken when we first met. She nods. We've talked about defining moments in her life—the first at age eight. She was never free to be innocent and her emotional growth was arrested by ongoing sexual trauma and abuse.

She's thirty-five. Physically she feels like she's eighty. In the outside world, her composure and behavior are that of a very successful professional. Emotionally/internally she's somewhere between eight and sixteen, depending on her feelings, stress, and level of anxiety.

She lives with PTSD, an anxiety disorder. She experiences vivid nightmares, flashbacks, and intrusive thoughts. She has co-occurring panic attacks and depression. Her prognosis is good and getting better, but the work ahead of her is hard. In truth, it's one of the most difficult things a human being can do—but it's not as bad as what she's already been through and it's not as bad as living this way indefinitely.

We're working on strategies to promote a sense of safety. She's implemented simple ways she can use her five senses (taste, touch, sight, smell, and sound) to connect to her here and now. She is mindful that when she's overwhelmed, she is not dealing with her current reality—she is somewhere in her past. She's making changes to her physical environment. She realized that even some of her prized possessions are associated with her past memories. They were in her bedroom when she was eight. They're packed away now—not discarded—it's just not time for those now.

We're working on a very difficult piece. She's begun journaling the content of her nightmares, and we're exploring the themes and the memories. She's accepted that the only way out of it is through it because there is no forgetting.

She's accepted that it's OK for a grown woman to leave her lights on at night, hug stuffed animals, and do anything that doesn't hurt her to make the "shadows" go away. She's getting better and through group therapy and self help she's connecting to others with similar experiences. She knows now that she's not alone.

Telling our stories connects us. The best we can be alone is lonely. "There is no greater agony than bearing an untold story inside you" —Maya Angelou.

PTSD Assessment Tests and First Steps

The following assessments are available online for post-traumatic stress disorder:

Source: Nebraska.gov:
http://www.ptsd.ne.gov/pdfs/ptsd.pdf

Source: BizCalcs:
http://mentalhealth.bizcalcs.com/Calculator.asp?Calc=Post-Traumatic-Stress

Source: My Healthy Place:
http://www.healthyplace.com/psychological-tests/ptsd-test/

Source: Veterans PTSD and Mental Health Guide
http://communitywarvets.org/ptsdtest.htm

First Steps Toward Healing

1. Recognize that the symptoms of PTSD are *normal reactions to abnormal circumstances*. Although you may feel like you are out of control or "going crazy," in reality, you are experiencing PTSD symptoms that make sense for the disorder.

2. Talk about your thoughts, feelings, and reactions to the events with people you trust and who understand the process and the symptoms. Keep a journal to help process your thoughts and feelings.

3. Take steps to create a feeling of safety and peace in your immediate environment. For instance, sleep with a nightlight, listen to music when you go to sleep, learn to meditate or do deep breathing exercises.

4. Resume your normal activities as quickly as possible after the event or take steps to reestablish your routine. Traumatic events can cause feelings of chaos. Routine and structure help create feelings of safety, normalcy, and security as you heal.

5. Treat yourself like a recovering patient. Rest, eat nutritious food, and exercise. Trauma takes an enormous toll on your body. Focus on restoration.

6. Practice advocacy for yourself or ask someone to do it on your behalf. Does a perpetrator need to be prosecuted? Do you need someone to accompany you for trauma treatment? Do you need to take the first steps toward addiction recovery? Take positive action toward recovery and healing, and ask for help if you feel you can't do it alone. Record your struggles and your progress in a journal.

7. Become aware of your triggers (sights, sounds, songs, smells, activities, places, people, etc.), and learn to cope with them. Talk with a trauma specialist who can help you create strategies. Practice positive self-talk (for example, "This scares me, but I know I'm safe").

8. Look for deeper significance and purpose in what happened to you. Even though you experienced something painful, you

survived and can use your experience in a positive way. What have you learned? How can you use this to help others? Record your thoughts in your journal or find an outlet for speaking hope into the lives of others.

9. Seek therapy with a trauma specialist. The good news is that PTSD is treatable. Find a counselor who understands the unique impact of trauma on the brain, rather than implementing a typical counseling approach. You can find a list of recommendations in appendix 3. If you were a crime victim, most states offer victims assistance to pay for psychotherapy. For more information call the National Organization for Victim Assistance at 800-879-6682.

10. Be patient with yourself. Healing takes time and doesn't take place in a straight line. Expect ups and downs in your healing—it's part of the process. Refuse to define yourself as a victim, and commit to emerging stronger and with a greater intimacy with God.

Resources

Note: The authors are not trained in medical or psychiatric care. This list does not constitute an endorsement by the authors of the content, methods, message, or effectiveness of the resource. If you have concerns or questions, consult with your own health care provider or certified counselor.

Resource & Information Websites

American Foundation for Suicide Prevention (http://www.afsp.org/). The nation's leading organization bringing together people across communities and backgrounds to understand and prevent suicide, and to help heal the pain it causes.

Celebrate Recovery (http://www.celebraterecovery.com). A biblical and balanced program that helps us overcome our hurts, hang-ups, and habits. It is based on the actual words of Jesus rather than psychological theory.

Cloud-Townsend Resources (http://www.cloudtownsend.com). Helps people grow and reach their goals personally, professionally, spiritually, and relationally.

Cradle My Heart (www.CradleMyHeart.org). Cradle My Heart offers post-abortion trauma resources, to help women find God's love after abortion.

Daughters of Destiny (www.DaughtersofDestiny.org). Equips, trains, and empowers volunteers to reach and disciple incarcerated women for Jesus while in prison and upon release.

FOCUS Ministries (http://www.focusministries1.org). Offers domestic violence and domestic abuse help for women and families. FOCUS stands for *focus on Christ for ultimate satisfaction.*

Focus on the Family (www.FocusontheFamily.com). A global Christian ministry dedicated to helping families thrive. Some available resources include:

Life Challenges Topics
- Understanding Emotional Abuse
- Battling Drug and Alcohol Abuse
- Conquering Cutting and Other Forms of Self-Injury
- Sexual Abuse
- Eating Disorders

Emotional Health Topics
- Living without Constant Guilt
- Changing an Angry Spirit
- Stress
- Depression

Topics Related to Love and Sex
- Pornography
- Abortion

Topics Related to Relationship Challenges
- Learning to Forgive
- Dealing with Physical Distance in Marriage
- Conflict Resolution

GriefShare (http://www.griefshare.org). Biblically based groups and support resources for those going through death-related grief.

Heal My PTSD (www.HealMyPTSD.com). Support, education, and information about post-traumatic stress disorder.

Help for My Life (www.helpformylife.org). Faith-based resources that help people grapple with the various struggles of life, from abuse to addiction, parenting to PTSD.

Human Life Services (www.HumanLifeServices.org). Offers post-abortion care.

ICORVI Ministries (http://icorvi.org). Faith-based facilitative conciliation services and training.

Make the Connection (http://maketheconnection.net). Shared experiences and support for veterans.

Mommies with Hope (http://mommieswithhope.com). Biblically based support for women who have experienced the loss of an infant.

Music for the Soul (http://musicforthesoul.org). A Christian ministry that uses the power of song and story as a bridge to hope and healing for those facing life's most difficult issues.

PTSDPerspectives (www.PTSDPerspectives.org). The authors' website that offers continuing education for medical and other professionals, and includes a blog that covers a variety of PTSD-related topics.

Sidran Institute (www.sidran.org). Traumatic stress education and advocacy.

Trauma Focused Cognitive Behavioral Therapy, Medical University of South Carolina (www.tfcbt.musc.edu)

U.S. Department of Veterans Affairs, National Center for PTSD (www.PTSD.va.gov). To advance the clinical care and social welfare of America's veterans and others who have experienced trauma, or who suffer from PTSD, through research, education, and training.

The VA PTSD Program Locator, for finding help in your area: http://www2.va.gov/directory/guide/ptsd_flsh.asp

Crisis Hotlines

Make the Connection (www.MaketheConnection.net/resources). Shared experiences and support for veterans.

National Domestic Violence Hotline: 1.800.799.7233. Offers confidential support 24/7. For those with a speech or hearing impairment who have TTY equipment, call 1-800-787-3224.

National Sexual Assault Hotline: 1.800.656.HOPE. At any given moment, more than 1,100 trained volunteers are on duty and available to help victims at RAINN-affiliated crisis centers across the country. RAINN (Rape, Abuse, and Incest National Network; http://www.rainn.org/) carries out programs to prevent sexual violence, help victims, and ensure that rapists are brought to justice.

National Suicide Prevention Lifeline (1.800.273.TALK). This national network will call the crisis center closest to your location.

Options are offered for veterans (press 1) and Spanish speakers (press 2). For those with a speech or hearing impairment who have TTY equipment, call 1-800-799-4TTY.

S.A.F.E. Alternatives (1.800.DONTCUT; http://www.selfinjury .org/). SAFE is an acronym for Self Abuse Finally Ends, and it's committed to helping individuals achieve an end to self-injurious behavior.

Books

Breaking Invisible Chains: The Way to Freedom from Domestic Abuse
by Susan Osborn, Jeenie Gordon, and Karen Kosman (New Hope, 2013)

Cradle My Heart: Finding God's Love After Abortion
by Kim Ketola (Kregel, 2012)

Cut: Mercy for Self-Harm
by Nancy Alcorn (WinePress, 2007)

Healing the Scars of Emotional Abuse (other titles as well)
by Dr. Gregory Jantz (Revell, 2009)

Heavenly Relationships Start on Earth
by attorney David W. Garrett (ICORVI Consulting, 2005)

Hope for Today, Promises for Tomorrow: Finding Light Beyond the Shadow of Infant Loss or Miscarriage
by Teske Drake (Kregel, 2012)

Inside a Cutter's Mind: Understanding and Helping Those Who Self-Injure
by Jerusha Clark (NavPress, 2007)

Precious Lord, Take My Hand: Meditations for Caregivers
by Shelly Beach (Discovery House, 2007)

Refuge: A Pathway Out of Domestic Violence and Abuse
by Donald Stewart (New Hope Publishers, 2004)

Rise Above Abuse: Victory for Victims of Five Types of Abuse
by June Hunt (Harvest House, 2010)

A Search for Purple Cows: A True Story of Hope
by Susan Call (Guideposts, 2013)

The Silent Seduction of Self-Talk
by Shelly Beach (Moody Publishers, 2009)

Sober Mercies: How Love Caught Up with a Christian Drunk
by Heather Kopp (Jericho Books, 2013)

The Spirit-Led Life: Christianity and the Internal Family System
Mary K. Steege and Richard C. Schwartz (CreateSpace, 2010)

The Truth About Trauma
Shelly Beach and Wanda Sanchez
PTSDPerspectives.org (free e-book)

When a Man You Love Was Abused
by Cecil Murphey (Kregel, 2012)

When a Woman You Love Was Abused
by Dawn Scott Jones (Kregel, 2013)

Treatment Centers

Intensive Trauma Therapy (www.TraumaTherapy.us / 304.291.2912)

The Center, A Place of Hope (www.aplaceofhope.com / 800.240.4354)

Pine Rest Christian Mental Health Services (http://www.pinerest .org/home / 800.678.5500)

Note: *The authors would like to note that Wanda Sanchez underwent several modes of therapy, along with biblical counseling, as well as treatment in various clinical settings over the course of more than forty years. She saw limited improvement in her trauma symptoms until she went to Intensive Trauma Therapy in Morgantown, West Virginia, for ten days of outpatient treatment under the Instinctual Trauma Response (IRT) modality of therapy. In just days, her nightmares, flashbacks, obsessions, and other symptoms vanished or radically diminished, and other aspects of Wanda's PTSD became manageable. We are strong advocates of the ITR model and Intensive Trauma Therapy because of their extremely effective means of achieving life-changing results in a minimal amount of time.*

How to Help Your Medical Provider Understand PTSD

Medical providers work hard to give their patients the best care possible, but they often don't understand the implications of post-traumatic stress disorder from a patient's perspective. Simple procedures may be triggering to you but seem harmless or even helpful to a health care provider.

You might consider writing a short letter to your doctor prior to your visit to briefly explain how PTSD impacts your patient experience. Or you may want to make a few verbal requests at an appointment or have someone make them for you. It's not necessary for you to go into all the details of your story. A diagnosis of PTSD can have implications for insurance companies, so be sure to find out whether or not that terminology becomes a part of your medical record with your health care provider.

Many medical communities are moving toward a trauma-informed care model. Ask your doctor if he or she is familiar with trauma-informed care. It is common for health providers to make reasonable accommodations for patients.

Reasonable accommodations include:

- Allowing you to wait in an alternate location other than a crowded waiting room
- Allowing the presence of an advocate with you during appointments
- Using female personnel when possible
- Minimizing undressing and gowning
- Not approaching you from behind or otherwise surprising you with touch; instead, ask first (for instance, "Is it okay if I place the stethoscope on your chest now?")
- Eliminating or minimizing unnecessary procedures (for instance, forbidding medical students to use you to learn how to give bed baths)
- Giving warm-up appointments for stressful exams (for instance gynecological or breast exams)
- Allowing premedication when needed to make procedures more tolerable (e.g., laughing gas for dental appointments or sedatives for triggering procedures)

Be sure to approach your physician respectfully. If you are triggered at an appointment, write a follow-up letter that briefly explains your experience and request a reasonable accommodation. For instance, if eye procedures trigger you, request premedication. If you discover that your anxiety increases as you wait in a crowded waiting room for your eyes to dilate, ask if you can wait in an exam room with a friend. If the doctor approaches you from behind and triggers you, ask if a friend could sit at your side and explain the doctor's movements before he or she touches you.

Suggestions for Friends, Spouses, and the Church

Someone you know and care about has been touched by trauma—people who sit beside you at basketball games, in the boardroom, or in your church pew. People you work with or who live around the corner or next door. Your child's teacher, your mechanic, or your manicurist.

Seventy percent of adults in the United States have experienced some kind of traumatic event in their lifetime, and approximately 8 percent of the general population is dealing with effects of post-traumatic stress disorder at some level.

Many of these people are struggling, and they don't know why. They're unsure how to get through one more day. Many are dealing with the symptoms of PTSD and turning to the coping mechanisms that help them deal with the pain: cutting, burning, substance abuse, obsessive behaviors. Many people feel guilty and ashamed about turning to these behaviors and don't know where to turn for help. Unfortunately, those coping mechanisms wear out and eventually stop working.

When they do stop working, many people become desperately depressed and consider suicide.

How can you help?

Everything we, Wanda and Shelly, do in life is motivated by our faith. We believe we're called to be hope carriers for those who have lost hope and to be light in a dark world. As believers in Jesus Christ, we're called to love others as we want to be loved ourselves, but that can be tough in a world where people abuse others and where trauma is a part of life. So how do we do this?

1. **By understanding.** We show compassion by learning about trauma and PTSD, its causes, treatments, and effects. We show we care when we understand that those who struggle with PTSD often struggle with guilt and shame for the things done to them and for the coping mechanisms they turn to in order to survive the pain. They need compassion and understanding that flows from a genuine spirit of love.

2. **By listening without judgment or easy answers.** Life is complicated and messy, and it's insincere to offer simplistic answers for every hurt. People who've experienced trauma and abuse need the freedom to say life hurts, to say that they're afraid, and to know they're safe to express their feelings without being judged, given timelines, or fearing their pain will be spiritualized or minimized.

3. **By providing an environment of emotional safety.** This means talking about mental health issues openly and honestly in churches and faith settings and offering resources for emotional and prayer support, as well as guidance to professional counseling and needed therapy. Mental-health treatment does not diminish or threaten the authority of the Bible.

4. **By talking about the pain of life openly and in healthy ways.** People need to know that trauma is part of the broken world that Jesus came to save. They're not alone. They're not unfixable. Their symptoms make sense. They make sense. They have a reason to hope. But they will never know these things until we talk about difficult issues openly and honestly in our churches, communities, and families.

5. **By becoming knowledgeable about resources and pointing people to them.** Learn about local options for trauma treatment, as well as the best options nationally (see appendix 3). Various approaches exist for PTSD treatment (see Common Therapy Approaches in appendix 1).

6. **By being patient.** We can't expect everyone to heal in the same way, and people with PTSD move forward on different timelines. The circumstances of their wounding produce different factors for healing. Be patient. Don't impose your limited perspective onto their healing. Pray for them and with them. Direct them to appropriate resources. Ask them what support looks like to them. And never quit loving them in ways they can see and feel, as God directs you.

APPENDIX 6

Scriptural Affirmations

The Character of God

God is love.
  1 John 4:8

God's love endures forever.
  1 Chronicles 16:34

God loves me and approves of me.
  1 John 4:16; 2 Timothy 2:15

I can approach God confidently and talk to him. He hears me and responds to my prayers.
  1 John 5:14–15

God works *all things* together for my good.
  Romans 8:28–32

God listens to my prayers and answers them.
  Psalm 4:3

God is faithful and always keeps his word.
  Psalm 89:8

Nothing and no one can stop God's plan or defeat him.
  Deuteronomy 20:4; 1 Corinthians 15:57

God is the only source of reality.
   Psalm 14:1

Jesus is the source of my victory.
   1 Corinthians 15:57

Jesus will never leave me.
   Matthew 28:20

I trust in God because he alone is worthy of my trust.
   Isaiah 50:10

God wants me to be happy and loves to help me.
   Psalm 107

God loves to bless me.
   Matthew 7:11

God wants to answer my prayers, so I will be hopeful and wait expectantly.
   1 John 5:14–15

God fights my battles for me.
   2 Timothy 4:18; 1 Peter 5:7

God will heal my broken heart.
   Psalms 34:18; 147:3

God is always with me, and he's with me right now.
   1 John 4:16; 2 John 1:9

God was with me before I was born, and he will be with me when I die.
   Romans 8:38–39

God is powerful enough to do anything.
   Matthew 19:26

God's love and sovereignty encompass the past, present, and future. He always was and always will be.

Job 36:26; Jeremiah 29:11

Jesus is the only perfect human.

Romans 3:10, 23

God's Word and Jesus' Word are my final authority.

Matthew 17:5; 2 Timothy 3:16

God is generous. He gives me everything I need or desire, as long as those things are for my good.

John 16:24; 1 John 5:14–15

God is compassionate, just, righteous, and loving.

Jeremiah 9:24

God will provide for all my needs.

Romans 8:32

God watches over me, hears my cry, and comes to my rescue.

Psalm 145:17–20

God hates sin because it hurts me and all his children.

Mark 9:47

God will never leave me or forsake me.

Hebrews 13:5–6

God will never disappoint me.

Romans 5:3; Ephesians 3:20

Life is not fair, but God is just.

Jeremiah 9:23–24

I cannot always trust people, but I can always trust God.
    Proverbs 3:5–6

My True Identity

God loves me because he created me and I am his child.
    Matthew 7:11; Galatians 4:7

God loves me unconditionally, in spite of my imperfections.
    Romans 5:8

I am God's beloved and precious one.
    Jeremiah 31:3; John 3:16

I am spiritually blessed.
    Proverbs 16:16; Ephesians 1:3

I am valuable and priceless.
    Proverbs 12:6–7

I am striving to grow into maturity in godliness in mind and
character and to reach the proper measure of virtue and integrity in
order to reflect the image of my heavenly Father.
    Matthew 5:48

I love God.
    1 John 5:3; 2 John 1:6

I will wait humbly for God to promote my cause.
    James 4:10

Because of Jesus' death on the cross, I have free access to God.
    1 Peter 2:3–5

God has a good and perfect plan for my life.
    Jeremiah 29:11

Because God loves me, I love myself.
Mark 12:30–31

God calls me beautiful, and I am beautiful.
Genesis 1:27; Psalm 139:14; Ecclesiastes 3:11

God has blessed me with everything I need to fulfill his will for my life.
2 Peter 1:3

God will give me the desire and power to do what pleases him.
Philippians 2:13

I am not responsible for changing other people; God is.
Matthew 19:26

God began a good work in me, and he will finish what he has started.
Philippians 1:6

God created me to partner with him in his plan for the world and to do good works.
Ephesians 2:10

God is working to help me become more and more like Jesus until he comes again.
Romans 8:29; Philippians 1:6

No one and nothing can get in the way of God's plan for me.
Joshua 23:14

God doesn't withhold any good thing from me.
Psalm 84:11

As God's child, I am a peacemaker.
Matthew 5:9

God will not give me what I want—he will give me things that are much better.
   Ephesians 3:20

I will choose joy and hope and walk in the blessing of God.
   Proverbs 10:28; Proverbs 23:18

I choose to fear God and walk in holiness and purity.
   Acts 24:16; 1 John 5:3

I show God that I trust him when I obey him.
   1 Samuel 15:22

I won't let anger control me but will trust in God.
   Psalm 37:8–9

I will not be a slave to fear because I am a child of God, with all the rights and privileges that belong to Jesus.
   Romans 8:15; 2 Timothy 1:7

Everything in my life happens for a reason, often so I can learn.
   Ecclesiastes 3:1–17

Suffering and pain can lead me to God if I allow them to.
   Romans 5:3–5

My talents and abilities are gifts from God, and he will bless my efforts as I invest them for his use.
   Matthew 25:26–29; 1 Peter 4:10

Everything that belongs to God belongs to me.
   Galatians 4:7

I will be grateful, faithful, joyful, and hopeful.
   Psalm 132:16; Ecclesiastes 2:26; Colossians 1:11–12

God uses my problems to show his power and love and to increase my faith.
    John 11:4; Romans 8:28

I will wisely remove myself from relationships that damage the name of Jesus.
    Ephesians 5:11

No spiritual forces can be victorious over me when I obey God and his Word.
    Isaiah 54:17

My troubles will not last forever.
    Ecclesiastes 3:1–8; Luke 6:21

God gives me identity, acceptance, purpose, and security.
    Matthew 6:33; Romans 12:2

God is my refuge and fortress in time of trouble.
    Psalm 18:2; Matthew 19:26

I will walk in the Spirit and choose love, joy, peace, patience, goodness, faithfulness, kindness, gentleness, and self-control.
    Galatians 5:22–23

I will forgive and put the past behind me so I can move forward and heal.
    Ephesians 4:31–32

I am blessed with spiritual blessings that far outweigh material blessings.
    Galatians 5:22–23; 1 Timothy 6:6

Goodness and mercy will follow me all the days of my life, and I will dwell in the house of the Lord forever.
    Psalm 23:6

Forgiveness and Restoration

But even greater is God's wonderful grace and
his gift of forgiveness.
ROMANS 5:15 NLT

Seek forgiveness.
One of the thorniest and most difficult things we humans are ever called upon to do is to respond to evil with kindness and to forgive the unforgivable. Forgiving someone who has harmed us is a challenging process because forgiveness isn't a snapshot or photograph, it's a movie. Forgiveness is a process that takes time, that moves us through different seasons, and it doesn't happen in an instant.

A true heart of forgiveness is one that continually invites those who offend us to a deepening level of repentance and reconciliation, and we are called to forgive because we love reconciliation.

A heart that has truly forgiven is released to enjoy reconciliation and restoration.

> If my people, who are called by my name, will humble
> themselves and pray and seek my face and turn from their

wicked ways, then I will hear from heaven, and I will forgive their sin and will heal their land. (2 Chronicles 7:14)

Restoration is a process.
If we carry the banner of Christian, then we *are* his people and we *are* called by his name, right? At the dedication of the newly built temple, Solomon asked God for two things right off the bat for the people of Israel when they sinned: forgiveness and restoration. God told Solomon that when the Israelites sinned, they would be restored through a process. God's Word does not change, so this process can be successfully applied to our lives today:

• Humble ourselves.
Recognize our nothingness before God and acknowledge that on our own, we are both guilty and unworthy to be in his holy presence. It's *all* about God, not about us.

• Pray.
Prayer is an act of humility, *not* an opportunity to present God with a list of wants. He *does*, however, care about our needs and tells us to cast all our cares on Him (1 Peter 5:7). As we humble ourselves before God, we begin to discover his will for our lives through prayer.

• Seek his face (practice his presence).
Communion with God = seeking God's face. To seek his face is to live in his presence—to fellowship with him. Prayer is communion with God, and Scripture instructs us to seek him continually (1 Chronicles 16:11; Psalms 27:8; 105:4).

God wants us to walk with him the way that Enoch did, in such close fellowship that the line between earth and heaven becomes blurred. He wants to lead us every step of the way, from humility into prayer, and from prayer into communion with him.

• Turn in repentance.

Spiritual restoration involves repentance, which means that we turn from our wicked ways. The offspring of repentance is communion, but this is not the same repentance that is a prerequisite for salvation. This passage was addressed to "my people, who are called by my name," which means that God was addressing those who are already in the fold. Repentance for believers is transformation by a renewing of our minds (Romans 12:2).

Acknowledgments

From Shelly:
To my husband, Dan, whose support makes my writing and ministry possible. I love you, and you constantly amaze me with a rock-steady love that is my shelter, comfort, and delight. To my fantabulous children, who bring me immeasurable joy: Jessica and son-in-love, Mosiah; Nate and daughter-in-love, Allison, and sweet grandson, Gabe.

To my best friend, Wanda Sanchez, who has taught me more about grace and loving God than books can contain. Thank you for inviting me into your life.

To the women of the Guild, my writing comrades-in-arms and stretcher-bearers: Cynthia Beach, Angela Blycker, Ann Byle, Sharron Carrns, Lorilee Craker, Tracy Groot, and Alison Hodgson.

From Wanda:
To my parents, Daddy and Mom and Lil One (mother) and Pops: I am so proud to call myself your daughter. Each of you is burned into my heart forever, and I will esteem and honor you all the days of my life. I love you so very much—thank you for everything.

To my grandma, Louise Sanchez: Thank you for always being there for us. You are the one person who can always make me smile. I love you with all my heart.

To the *most* awesome sisters and brothers that anyone could wish for: Chris, Dawn, Lisa, Matt, Steve, Samuel, David, and Marc. I love you all and am so proud to be your big sister.

To Diana Chaparro and my cousin Carmen Torres: I have been blessed and honored with our years of friendship, and I am so proud of you. I love you and am honored that you let me sing with you. I can't wait to do it again!

To the Salsedo and Sanchez families (and all of the extensions of these families, too): I am humbled to call you family. I love you all.

To Keith Ortiz: You have been such an awesome cousin/big brother. You are one of my heroes, Keith. Your bravery in stepping up and speaking out in order to heal your soul and help others has been such a motivation to me to speak out more and share my story. Some of my story is in this book. Thank you for being who you are. I love you.

Many thanks and much love to the Templo de la Cruz family and friends; KFAX-AM1100 family; Dawn Scott Jones, for your friendship and guidance; Miss Monika, for teaching me to play; my friend and teacher, Miss Liza Kendall Christian; Caroll F. and Nancy S., Lucy M., Becky Escalante, and Kim de Blecourt.

To my cousin Ruth Wilson, thank you for always understanding me and never judging me. Thank you for being like a big sister to me. I love you, Ruthie.

To Craig Roberts: My friend and the best broadcast journalist I have ever worked with, and the host of *Lifeline.* Thank you for years of friendship and for teaching me so much about what a good leader is.

To Eddie: Thank you for introducing me to Shelly Beach . . . what great instinct on your part! You always did have wonderful instincts, among your gazillion gifts. I hope that somewhere in this world you will read this book and know that you really wrote the first page. I love you, sweet friend, and pray that someday we will meet again.

To Shelly, my coauthor, friend, and teacher: Who could have ever imagined where this was going when you first answered God's heart-tug to call a woman you didn't know? You were an answer to my less-than-eloquent prayer, "Help!" I will be forever grateful to you for diving into my life before even knowing the details. God has burned you into my heart forever. Thank you for teaching me. I love you.

And finally, to my Hope, my Redeemer, my God, I give you thanks. It's *all* about you, and I love you with my whole heart.

From both of us:
To the great staff at Kregel Publications and their extraordinary efforts on behalf of this book: Dennis Hillman, publisher; Steve Barclift, acquisitions and managing editor; Becky Durost Fish, Dawn Anderson, and Leah Mastee, our editors, who made the editing process a delight and whose insights were hugely appreciated; Noelle Pedersen and Adam Ferguson, our marketing and promotional team; and Nick Richardson and Sarah Slattery, the book's designers.

Thank you to the life-changing teaching ministry of Blythefield Hills Church and its culture of transparency, accountability, discipleship, and commitment to the Word.

To the amazing staff at Intensive Trauma Therapy in Morgantown, West Virginia, who gave us the tools for healing and the courage to speak healing into the lives of others.

To our amazing families who support us as we write into the wee hours, travel the country speaking, and continue our never-ending search for the best cupcake in the USA.

To Julianne Paulsen: Thank you for your investment in our lives and ministry. We love you.

About the Authors

SHELLY BEACH is a Christy Award–winning author of ten books, as well as a writing consultant and adjunct professor at Cornerstone University. She is cofounder of the Breathe Christian Writers Conference in Grand Rapids, Michigan, and the Cedar Falls Christian Writers Workshop in Cedar Falls, Iowa. Together with Wanda Sanchez, she is cofounder of PTSDPerspectives.org and consults nationally in prisons, hospitals, and mental health facilities. She also speaks at conferences and seminars on mental health and spiritual formation.

Shelly first became interested in the topic of trauma and post-traumatic stress disorder when she began researching the topic on a search to address symptoms of family members, as well as her own symptoms stemming from an assault by a serial rapist when she was nineteen years old. During her investigation, she learned about a life-changing treatment that had worked for the son of a writing colleague.

Days later, a series of miracles prompted Shelly to call Wanda Sanchez—a stranger who lived half a continent away and whom Shelly had never met. What transpired over the next months and years was a miracle of healing, as well as a friendship, that only God could orchestrate.

Shelly can be found at shellybeachonline.com.

With more than twenty years of broadcast media experience in radio and television, **WANDA SANCHEZ** is executive producer of the longest running radio talk show in the northern California/San Francisco market. She is the cofounder of PTSDPerspectives.org and consults nationally in prisons, hospitals, and mental health facilities. She also speaks at conferences and seminars on mental health, hope, and healing.

Although Wanda's career meant daily contact with top-ranking national and world political icons, cultural giants, entertainers, and Christian leaders, she lived a secret life hidden from public view. As a child, she experienced ongoing physical, emotional, and sexual abuse at the hands of multiple perpetrators. Over the years, her symptoms of post-traumatic stress disorder escalated. By the time she reached her late forties, she'd tried various forms of counseling, rehab, and therapy approaches—with little or no success.

In 2010, Wanda was days away from implementing a suicide plan when a stranger on the other side of the country called her and told her that her symptoms not only made sense, but that trauma treatment could help her. Within months, Shelly Beach accompanied Wanda for intensive trauma therapy that radically changed her life. Today the two women are best friends, PTSD consultants, and coauthors.

Wanda lives in the Grand Rapids, Michigan, area and can be found at www.PTSDPerspectives.org.